J. BERNAUER
UDAC

M000310514

Casting Nets
and
Testing Specimens

Casting Nets
and
Testing Specimens

TWO GRAND METHODS OF PSYCHOLOGY

Philip J. Runkel

PRAEGER

New York
Westport, Connecticut
London

Library of Congress Cataloging-in-Publication Data

Runkel, Philip Julian, 1917–
    Casting nets and testing specimens : two grand methods of
psychology / by Philip J. Runkel.
        p.   cm.
    Includes bibliographical references.
    ISBN 0-275-93533-7 (alk. paper)
    1. Psychology—Statistical methods. 2. Psychology, Experimental.
3. Psychology—Research—Methodology.   I. Title.
BF39.R78   1990
150′.72—dc20   89-48665

Copyright © 1990 by Philip J. Runkel

All rights reserved. No portion of this book may be
reproduced, by any process or technique, without the
express written consent of the publisher.

Library of Congress Catalog Card Number: 89-48665
ISBN: 0-275-93533-7

First published in 1990

Praeger Publishers, One Madison Avenue, New York, NY 10010
An imprint of Greenwood Publishing Group, Inc.

Printed in the United States of America

The paper used in this book complies with the
Permanent Paper Standard issued by the National
Information Standards Organization (Z39.48-1984).

10 9 8 7 6 5 4 3 2 1

Copyright Acknowledgments

The author and publisher are grateful to the following for allowing the use of excerpts from:

S. W. Cook. The origins of action research. *SAFT Newsletter*, 1(3) (Summer 1987): 1–2. Used by permission of the Society for the Advancement of Field Theory.

R. E. Kaplan, M. M. Lombardo, and M. S. Mazique. A mirror for managers: Using simulation to develop management teams. *Journal of Applied Behavioral Science*, 21(3) (1985): 241–53. Used by permission of JAI Press.

D. Krech and R. S. Crutchfield. *Theory and problems of social psychology*. New York: McGraw-Hill, 1948. Copyright 1948 by McGraw-Hill. Used by permission.

R. S. Marken. Intentional and accidental behavior: A control theory analysis. *Psychological Reports*, 50 (1982): 647–50. Used by permission.

R. S. Marken. Perceptual organization of behavior: A hierarchical control model of coordinated action. *Journal of Experimental Psychology: Human Perception and Performance*, 12(3) (1986): 267–76. Copyright 1986 by the American Psychological Association; adapted by permission of the publisher and author.

W. T. Powers. A systems approach to consciousness. In J. Davidson and R. Davidson (eds.), *The Psychobiology of consciousness*. New York: Plenum, 1980. Used by permission.

S. S. Stevens and M. Guirao. Individual loudness functions. *Journal of the Acoustical Society of America*, 36 (1964): 2210–13. Used by permission of the American Institute of Physics.

G. Szamosi. *The twin dimensions: Inventing time and space*. New York: McGraw-Hill, 1986. Copyright 1986 by McGraw-Hill. Used by permission.

The presuppositions of science
are normally mistaken for its findings.

E. F. Schumacher,
Small is beautiful:
Economics as if people mattered

Contents

Acknowledgments

I once read a book in which, in the preface, the author named all the people he claimed had helped him to shape his thoughts. He started before Aristotle and ran on for seven or eight pages. No doubt he was reasonably correct, but he was also a bore.

I would not have been able to get my thoughts about current research method into a shape that would have left me reasonably satisfied without having read the writings of Wm. T. Powers. I am grateful to him, too, for reading several versions of the entire manuscript, for pointing out parts that needed fixing, and for helping me with the mathematics. I am grateful to Carol Slater for introducing me to the literature on natural kinds and for scrutinizing my assumptions lurking behind the assumptions that I claim lurk within research methods.

Several other kind people read the whole manuscript: Gerald K. Bogen, J. Thomas Hastings, Daniel Langmeyer, Frederick F. Lighthall, Richard S. Marken, Robert J. Menges, Mary Powers, Richard J. Robertson, Carol Slater, Leona E. Tyler, and Greg Williams. Several kind people read parts: Twila Abbott, Diane M. Dunlap, Joseph E. McGrath, Laurence D. Richards, Richard A. Schmuck, P. J. Slack, Robert Smith, and Thomas Tinsley. All those people made helpful comments. I am grateful to them. I am very grateful to Dieter Frey and Dagmar Stahlberg for actually encouraging me to subject an article of theirs to detailed criticism in Chapter 4; I admire greatly both their generosity and their scholarly stance. I am grateful to Mary Claire Runkel for her careful scrutiny of clarity and logic and for her hand-in-hand aid with every detail of the final manuscript.

Casting Nets
and
Testing Specimens

1

Overview

We all gather information, every day, every moment, squirreling it away in our memories. We gather information whether we are reading, crossing a street, digging in the garden, interviewing a political condidate, painting a picture, or conducting a psychological experiment. Sometimes we use the information in the next split second, sometimes next year.

We use various methods to gather information and so to come to beliefs about the behavior of ourselves and others. Our methods are often very sophisticated when we act as social scientists, and are often rough and ready when we act in ordinary life, but we all use methods of some sort, and we often cite them to justify our beliefs. We say, "I saw her do it," or "We queried 1,500 randomly selected households." This book is about the methods we choose by means of which to reach conclusions. It is about how we come to beliefs about the nature and behavior of humans and other living creatures.

Despite the long list of particular methods and the names social scientists have given them, almost all fall into one of two grand classes that I will call the *method of relative frequencies* (to be explained in Chapters 2 through 8) and the *method of specimens* (to be explained in Chapters 9 through 12). Both methods can deliver useful information about human behavior. The main point of this book, however, will be to show that for a long time now most social scientists have been using the method of relative frequencies for the wrong purpose—to discover how the human animal, as a species, functions. The method that can do that is the method of specimens. To assert once more, however, my claim that both methods have their suitable uses, I will explain *action research*, in Chapter 13, as a very useful amalgam of the two methods.

Though I think all the methods that have names and self-conscious procedures turn out to be varieties of either the method of relative frequencies or the method of specimens, I think the greatest amount of information-getting, if we count by person-hours, is done simply by finding out whether something can happen—whether something is possible. We can do that without adhering to any rules and without any intent to "generalize." I call that kind of information-seeking the *method of possibilities* and explain it in Chapter 13.

I will say, as I go along, that the secrets of the behavior of humans and other living creatures will not be uncovered by counting noses—by the method of relative frequencies. They will not yield to the sophisticated procedural apparatus that statisticians and social scientists have built during this century on the foundations laid by Galton, Pearson, and Fisher—the apparatus that includes random sampling, control groups, correlations, analysis of variance, factor analysis, discriminant analysis, and multidimensional scaling. The secrets of behavior will continue to emerge, as they have in the past, from the method of specimens.

I will not say that information gathered by random sampling, counting noses, and statistical analysis has no use. The method of relative frequencies is very good indeed for making catalogs or maps, so to speak—for making good guesses about where or under what conditions certain kinds of behavior are likely to occur and the proportions in which they are likely to occur. That is a valuable thing to be able to do.

If I take more space in this book explaining what the method of relative frequencies *will not* do than I take telling what it *will* do, I do so to redress the balance. I think most of the books on the library shelves about polling and social surveys are largely right in what they say. But I think that most texts offered for academic courses in research method in psychology and other social sciences are largely wrong, including the book that I wrote with my friend Joseph McGrath (Runkel and McGrath, 1972).

I am not the only one, of course, to complain about the current canons of research method. For several decades, the literature has included declarations of discontent. For example, Gergen and Morawski in 1980 gave a concise review of several lines of thought about the inadequacies of method in social psychology; their core comments applied equally well to other social sciences. In 1986, Thorngate and also Cairns gave cogent examples of some ways that widely used research strategies lead researchers into wrong conclusions about individuals.

Many social scientists nowadays seem to believe that good theory will be built if only we can sufficiently refine the current canons of research method and persuade enough colleagues to cling to them rigorously. But the assumptions underlying the current canons do not fit the purpose to which many social scientists try to bend the canons. No matter how carefully you sharpen the teeth of a saw or how neatly you fit it with a new handle, it will remain a poor instrument for driving nails.

I will also argue that we can conceive causation in two ways: as linear input-to-output or as circular. By circular, I do not mean repetitive or cyclic. I mean cause and effect in a fully connected loop such that at any moment any event in the loop can equally well be called a cause or an effect. I will explain these matters in Chapters 8 and 9. The method of relative frequencies typically rests on the metatheory of linear causation. The method of specimens typically requires the metatheory of circular causation.

TWO METHODS

It is easy to find highly predictable phenomena by looking either at (a) an individual's control of bodily purposes or (b) statistics of masses of people. We can predict that every person not suffering internal damage or disorder will maintain an internal temperature between very narrow limits. We cannot usually, however, predict very well the particular actions the person will take to maintain that temperature—whether the person will take in more fuel by eating and if so what or when, whether or when the person will put on a coat or a blanket or snuggle against another warm body or build a shelter or make a fire, or whether the person will exercise to increase the flow of warm blood to the bodily extremities. We cannot predict particular actions very well, but we can predict with certainty that *every* person will act to maintain a particular temperature. We can predict confidently that under the threat of cold weather, *everyone* will take *some* sort of easily visible action to aid the body in maintaining the desired internal temperature.

Statistics about mass phenomena, too, are often very reliable. The increases and decreases in traffic flow over the arterial streets of a city as rush hours come and go are highly predictable. So are seasonal change in retail purchasing and in visits to the Grand Canyon. The reliability of a mass phenomenon does not, however, enable us to predict well the behavior of any element of it. We are not helped to predict the time Clarence Berquistson will drive to work, what arterial he will choose, or whether he will visit the Grand Canyon this year. The proprieter of a drugstore cares little who comes in to buy vitamins, but does care how many do so. On the other hand, though the proprietor does not need to know much about the average pharmacist, he does need very much to know how to deal reliably with his own pharmacist, Clarence Berquistson.

Social scientists exhibit two needs similar to those of the drugstore proprietor. First, if social scientists want to know the proportions of individuals who will, with some specifiable probability, exhibit one sort of action in one sort of situation, they can then simply count anonymous cases, as do the druggist and the National Park Service. Culture and geography make it easier for people to carry out their purposes through certain uses of the environment instead of others. We can, therefore, predict not only that people in cold climates will do something to keep themselves warm, but also predict the proportions of people in a certain culture who will keep themselves warm by certain methods. This is the method of relative frequencies. Some of the success that researchers have in predicting frequencies of behavior at rates better than chance even among relatively small collections of subjects is due, if the researchers are careful to sample randomly, to this cultural predictability of mass behavior.

Second, if social scientists want to know how any and every individual functions, they must study the ways a neural net deals with sensory input, since sensory input is the only path through which a human or other living creature can know the environment and therefore initiate selective acts upon it. (By "neural net," I mean all the neural tissue in the body.) Psychophysicists, physiological psychologists, physiologists, neurologists, and other biological scientists do indeed study those neural functions that are the same over long periods of time in every undamaged individual. This is the method of specimens.

Both methods deliver useful information. Both enable us to generalize, to get ready for future events. They do so, however, differently. The method of relative frequencies enables us to anticipate statistics about collections of people. The method of specimens enables us to anticipate the perceptual inputs that a particular individual will act to maintain and the invariant processes by which individuals maintain their unique perceptual inputs.

The two methods deliver different kinds of information. The method of frequencies enables us to estimate behavioral trends in the mass—such as how many anonymous lemmings will run into the ocean this year. The method of specimens enables us to discover how a species "works"—how its internal workings enable it to do what it does.

THEMES

In addition to setting forth what the two chief methods can and cannot do, I will touch now and then on certain other themes.

Purpose

Throughout this book, I assume that humans act according to their purposes. If you do not think people have purposes, you may as well stop here.

Generalizing

I mean by this term predicting, anticipating, even getting ready for further action. I include conscious predicting in generalizing, but I also include unconscious readiness for the next occasion that requires action. I mean choosing an action that will (we think or hope) bring us what we want when we find ourselves in a similar situation.

Generalizing was not invented by scientists or statisticians. When we do it, and we do it all the time, we are doing what comes naturally. It is a necessary capability, an ever-present function of all living creatures.

When social scientists think about generalizing, they do not use an arcane logic more potent than the logic used by the rest of us. The logic and procedure of science come simply from the efforts of ordinary people trying their best to be careful when they think about what they observe and when they tell others about it. Attention to logic is necessary and important, but I think adhering with exquisite rigor to any cluster of canons encourages us to prize manner above meaning, wrapping above contents, ritual above substance.

Generalizing occurs in both everyday life and formal research. Generalizing in science may be typically more systematic, self-critical, and publicly inspected than in other realms of life (though I am not nearly as sure of that claim as I once was), but there is no discontinuity. Because that is my view, because I think we generalize both unconsciously and consciously and in everyday life as well as in the laboratory, I will offer in this book illustrations from everyday life as freely as I offer accounts of formal research.

Particular and General

We can generalize from the particular to the general in our minds—at the upper levels of the neural net. When we act, however, we can act only because we have generalized from the general to the particular. Any kind of research can serve a practical purpose if it gives us a guide to diagnosis.

Diagnosis

Generalizing cannot tell us with full certainty what to expect in the next hour or around the next corner even in principle. It cannot be a prescription for immediate, particular action. Even with the most reliable physical phenomena, we encounter surprises. We turn an ankle on a small stone. Dirt somehow gets between electrical connectors. A label reading "Sulfuric Acid" somehow gets on a bottle that actually contains something else. Generalizing serves us well only if we constantly keep diagnosing (testing) the present condition.

SUMMARY

I think we use two grand methods of strategies to get information from experience—to get ready to perceive future events and deal with them. I call one the method of relative frequencies. Using it, we count cases and estimate statistics. We look for ways in which conditions and actions cluster. In Chapters 2 through 8, I will show what I think the method of relative frequencies can do and what it cannot do.

The other method I call the method of specimens. Using it, we treat persons as members of a species. We look for features of behavior—the "rules" by which people choose behavior—that are invariant within an individual over time and that are the same from one person to another. We do not expect to find invariants in repeated particular actions, but in the inferred internal functioning that controls perceptions. I will say more about invariants in Chapter 9, and about circular causation, too. In Chapter 12, I will explain how the method of specimens can actually enable us to make working models of human behavior. Over the course of Chapters 9 through 12, I will show what I think the method of specimens can do and what it cannot do.

In Chapter 13, I will describe action research as a melding of the methods of relative frequencies and specimens. Also in Chapter 13, I will argue the merits of the "method" of possibilities—an informal but very useful strategy that lies outside the two main methods.

I

What the Method of Relative Frequencies Will Do

The method of relative frequencies is the method of choice for estimating the likelihood of finding any arbitrary countable actions associated with any arbitrary class of listable and countable persons—or other entities. It serves that purpose very well indeed. It is also useful for making catalogs, writing histories, and getting hints of internal standards. That is what Chapter 2 will cover.

For the accuracy of its estimates, the method relies unequivocally on random sampling. When sampling is carefully random, the method can estimate in a listed population, with calculable accuracy, not only proportions and means, but also relations among variables. It can even estimate, through the use of causal experiments, the likelihood that certain actions will follow presumed causes.

Random sampling, however, is sometimes very expensive. Worse than that, it is sometimes impossible. Researchers often feel driven, therefore, to nonrandom samples. Then they lose the power of the method of relative frequencies. But worst of all for the purposes of scientists who want to show forth the manner of functioning of the human animal, the method of relative frequencies is simply incapable of serving them. That is what Chapter 3 will cover.

2

Casting Nets

What I am calling the method of "relative frequencies" is the one in which the investigator tallies characteristics or actions of a good many, maybe a great many people—the kind of investigation given the most space by far in most texts on method in social science. It is the method around which has grown up the immense body of technique and lore that includes sampling techniques, statistical inference, regression analysis, rationales about control groups, various classifications of study designs, arguments over quantitative versus qualitative, and all the rest. To clarify the sort of study—and the sort of thinking—in which the method of relative frequencies underlies the conclusions drawn, I will describe in the first part of this chapter some guises in which the method appears. After that, I will explain what I think are the proper uses of the method.

The method of relative frequencies is the preeminent method of finding or locating things, for finding a place or condition where one kind of characteristic or action occurs more frequently than at another, for finding the lode, so to speak, rich in the characteristic or action you want. What proportion of registered voters say they intend to vote for Corcoran? Is the proportion larger in Georgia than in Michigan? With what variable X can we more often find people high on Y by picking people who are high on X? Do we find a larger proportion of tall people, in comparison to short people, in positions of leadership? Will parents who beat their children be found in greater proportion among those who themselves were beaten as children? Suppose a person's opinion is markedly different from the opinions of the others in a group; will we find that such persons are more likely (if we observe a hundred groups) to receive more communication than other members? What proportion of people in population P show characteristic C or take action A a short time after we increase the level of variable X?

SOME EXAMPLES

To carry my description further, I will divide studies using the method of relative frequencies into three kinds: polling, correlations, and causal experiments. I do not claim any virtue in dividing studies in that way; I do it only because those three kinds will have a familiar ring to most readers.

In polling (also called social surveying), the typical inquiry has this form: Among people in population P, what proportion are (or do) _____? In correlational studies, the typical inquiry has this form: Among people who are high (or moderate or low) on variable X, what proportion are high (or moderate or low) on variable Y? Correlational studies, of course, can be carried out by the methods of social surveys.

In causal experiments, the typical inquiry has this form: Among people who have (and have not) undergone the experience of _____, what proportions are (or do) _____? In the first part of that formula, you may, if you wish, substitute "who have undergone treatment A" or "who have been subjected to stimulus A," or any phrase you like to use to describe the intervention by the experimenter. The logic of causal experiments differs from that of correlational studies only on the point that in causal experiments, the experimenter does not take people as found, with their characteristics X and Y, as well as other unknown characteristics, having appeared in an unknown order before being assessed, and, furthermore, with many of the other characteristics confounding the interpretation of the correlation in unknown ways. Instead, the experimenter tests the order of causation by assessing the Y variable before assigning, randomly, portions of the subjects to different levels of the X variable, using the random assignment in the hope that the extraneous confounding variables will be distributed in an unbiased way.

A poll or social survey can be as simple as to inquire about only one variable, though it rarely is that simple. The other two types of studies ask about two or more variables. Complicated interlacings of variables are often investigated. For example, among people who are A, in comparison to those who are B, do we find an even larger proportion of people who are D when we look among those who are C?

In all varieties of what we call scientific research and in many varieties of everyday information-gathering, we study only a sample of those people we actually want to learn something about and then "generalize to" those we have not actually studied. (You might study your spouse diligently and systematically without intending to learn anything about anybody else, but few would describe that as scientific research.) In research, we always hope that the characteristics or patterns of behavior we see in the people we observe will reappear among some larger number of people we have not yet observed. The art of estimating the accuracy with which that happens is most highly developed in polling and survey research.

Polling

Polling is familiar to anyone who spends much time reading newspapers or watching television news programs. The technique is used in marketing, public health, criminology, political science, and many other fields. In polling, you hunt for the characteristic or the behavior you are curious about by first choosing a listable population and then selecting a sample. Of the persons in the sample, you ask a question such as "Do you like George Bush?" You need not always ask a question; you can instruct your interviewers to take note of something observable, such as whether the interviewees have radios in their living rooms. You figure the proportion of *yes*es. You then calculate that if you were to query or observe all the people in the listed population, the proportion of *yes*es would, with a certain probability, be within a certain number of percentage points of that in your sample. You generalize when you conclude that the probability is 95 percent that the proportion of *yes*es in the population is between, say, 57 and 63 percent.

When you sample randomly, generalization by the method of relative frequencies actually works. It has been tested empirically not only with red and black balls and with playing cards, but with real people. Many years ago, the U. S. Department of Agriculture conducted sample surveys and then compared their estimates with a census made soon afterward. The estimates were right on the button. Many similar tests have been made since. Obviously, polling and social surveys have very valuable practical applications.

Correlations

Correlations, too, tell you where things can be found clustered more densely. (I am using the term "correlation" loosely here to mean any kind of dependence among variables. I include contingency tables, as you will see below.) Here are a few examples, from the thousands one can find in the literature, of how correlations help us to find things. Mohandessi and Runkel discovered in Illinois in 1958 that secondary schools with higher mean scores on academic aptitude lay farther from coal mines, on the average, than those with lower. J. L. Brown (1987) reported studies showing that among people in the United States living at or below the official poverty level, a smaller portion of them were receiving food stamps in 1985 than in 1980. Cotton and Tuttle (1986) reported that turnover among employees was lower, on the average, in companies with unions than in those without. B. G. Fricke (1956) reported that the best way to find high school graduates who will do well in college is to take those with high academic rank in high school. After examining 22 studies of the behavior of college students and nonstudents (no two studies investigating the same kind of behavior), Gordon, Slade, and Schmitt (1986) reported that the average behavior of the students and nonstudents differed in three-quarters of the studies. After a project undertaken to develop stronger teamwork among the managers of a company, Kaplan, Lombardo, and Mazique (1985) reported the opinions of employees about their company before the project began and their changed opinions at two times afterward.

Luthans, Rosenkrantz, and Hennessey (1985) found interacting with outsiders, socializing, and politiking occurring more often among managers who were promoted more rapidly than among those promoted less rapidly. Koslowsky and Locke (1986) reported a way of classifying credit-card holders so as to find persons among which a proportion much greater than among all credit-card holders were likely to buy insurance by mail. Meyerhoff and White (1986) listed conditions in homes where, compared to other homes, a larger proportion of infants and young children were found to be smoothly developing skills with things and people. C. B. Schoonhoven (1981) showed how to find acute-care operating-room suites in hospitals in the United States with higher and lower rates of severe morbidity by using measures of the workflow uncertainty within the operating room and the destandardization, decentralization, professionalization, and resources of the hospital.

All those examples can be taken as instructions: "If you want to find concentrations of people who are or who do Y, look for people who are in condition X (or in a certain range of variable X)." Some of the studies were set up as causal experiments, but I take causal experiments to be a variant of correlations, just as I take correlations to be a variant of polling.

Polling tells you the proportion of certain kinds of people you can find in a population. If you divide the population into parts by using variable X, you can then observe the proportions of values of Y you find in those parts of X, and you have a correlation. If, instead of observing different people already to be found at the various levels of X, you yourself alter the levels of X among people you select, you then have a causal experiment.

Causal Experiments

Causal experiments find things for you in the same way that correlations do, but most researchers are more willing to make a claim about cause and effect after a causal experiment than after finding only a correlation. The essential reasoning goes like this. Suppose, for example, you find some sort of work that can be done either alone or in a group. You might ask people doing that kind of work how much they enjoy it. You might discover that, on the average, those who do the work in a group enjoy it more than those who work alone. Researchers would immediately worry that those persons who joined groups to do the work might have brought characteristics along with them that caused them to enjoy the work just as much or more than the mere fact of being in the group, while those who worked alone might have brought fewer of those characteristics to the work. To set up a causal experiment, researchers would find a batch of willing people and then randomly assign half to group work and half to individual work. The researchers would reason that the chance of getting people with other causal characteristics into the two assignments would be equal, and any difference in enjoyment would then be due to the difference between working in a group or alone. I will give a detailed example of a causal experiment in Chapter 4.

Instead of saying that the method of relative frequencies enables us to ascertain relations among variables, I have insisted that it is better to say that it enables us to find the greater densities, the richer lodes, of the characteristic or behavior we want to find. Beyond that, what I have said so far will no doubt have brought yawns of familiarity from some readers. But I wanted to make it clear that a very large portion of the work in social science uses what I call the method of relative frequencies. Some may say that I have now described the whole of method in social science. But the method of specimens is different. That will appear in Chapters 9 through 12.

WHAT THE METHOD OF RELATIVE FREQUENCIES WILL DO

What are the suitable uses of the method of relative frequencies? What can you do with it that you cannot do without it?

Casting a Net

The first thing you can do with the method of relative frequencies, a thing of great practical import, is what I will call casting a net. Having estimated from a sample of population A the proportion of people who have characteristic B, you can estimate how confident you should be of finding that proportion of B in your next sample of that population.

Fishermen want to know where and when they should cast their nets to maximize the catch. They want to cast their nets in the right part of the ocean and in the right season to catch the maximum number of fish. Mail-order houses that sell widgets want to know where to cast their mailings to catch the maximum number of people who are waiting breathlessly to buy widgets. Koslowsky and Locke (1986), whom I mentioned before, found ways to winnow credit-card holders so as to find a lode richer in people who would buy insurance policies by mail. They increased the purchasers from 0.2 to 0.6 percent. A percentage of only 0.6 seems small until you realize that the increase was threefold.

Police want to know where and when to station themselves to catch the maximum number of evil-doers. Organizations promoting causes want to know where to send their appeals to catch the maximum proportion of donors. Politicians want to know where and when to appear on television to appeal to the greatest proportion of undecided voters. Businesses want to know where and when to recruit employees so as to attract those with certain characteristics. And so on. That kind of use of random samples and relative frequencies can affect the flow of millions of dollars, the courses of millions of careers, and the satisfactions of millions of customers. The efficacy of that strategy has been demonstrated over and over again. That kind of generalization *works*.

The method of relative frequencies tells you about proportions and categories. Having inspected one sample, you can predict with as much accuracy as you wish (by enlarging your samples) the proportions of people in a second sample who will fall within specified ranges of any variable or combination of variables. (That statement, of course, assumes random sampling, and accuracy is limited by errors of measurement.) For any hypothesis you can conceive in relative-frequency form, you can get corroborating evidence in the form of predicted proportions in a second sample if only you observe the rules of random sampling and take large enough samples.

People who carry out opinion polls only rarely intend to check their generalizations later by counting the proportion in the entire population. If tallying the population were feasible (could be done speedily enough or at low enough cost), they would do that in the first place instead of taking a sample. Usually, the surveyors simply let their statements about the population rest on faith in the mathematics of probability. They recommend, for example, that their clients bet 20 to 1 that the population proportion will lie in the 95 percent confidence interval—an interval, for example, between the proportions of .57 and .63. Sometimes two surveys will be made on the same topic in the same population. If one survey predicts a 95 percent confidence interval between .57 and .63, and the other between .60 and .66, they vindicate each other, because the confidence intervals overlap.

Casting a net works with anonymity. If you do not care about catching some particular person, you can cast nets with great profit by using the method of relative frequencies. You can use it to benefit your business, campaign, or cause. Do not, however, count on the net to catch your son or daughter or best friend. The net does not know your best friend from anybody else.

The efficacy of any net lessens with time, because the statistical characteristics of any population change. To keep your net in good working order, you must take periodic samples to get current estimates of the population statistics. Any professional surveyor knows that.

Cataloging and Writing History

The second thing you can do with the method of relative frequencies is to compile natural histories and catalogs. This kind of casting about for similarities and differences can raise useful questions. It is useful to observe that the relative frequency of a particular species of bird is higher in Minnesota in June than in January. It prompts you to ask, "I wonder where all those others go in January?" It is useful to observe that in a temporary group of students, strangers to one another and talking about something not fatefully important to them, the person with the opinion most disparate from the rest draws the most communication. It prompts you to ask, "I wonder, leaving that person's disparity as it is, what might draw more communication to others in the group?"

Among the companies Cotton and Tuttle (1986) studied, they found that differences in turnover for sex, number of dependents, pay, and satisfaction with the work have become less pronounced in recent years. At the same time, the differences for union presence and sex were more pronounced in the United States than in other countries. That is an example of what I mean by natural history. Another good example is the study by Bronfenbrenner (1958), who inspected about 30 years of studies of the average permissiveness in child rearing. He found that the permissiveness of both lower-class and middle-class parents increased over the years, but the permissivenes of the middle-class parents increased faster on the average, and overtook that of the lower-class parents. Gergen (1973) has written persuasively about social psychology as history. Catalogs and histories are useful to sociologists, political scientists (perhaps politicians, too), and historians.

Hunting for Internal Standards

The third thing you can do with the method of relative frequencies is to look for kinds of internal standards you might find in some number of humans. By "internal standards," I mean kinds of goals, purposes, preferred states of being, yearnings, attitudes, beliefs—any of those internal images or criteria to which we want our actual experience to measure up. The method of relative frequencies cannot demonstrate an internal standard in any single person, but it can suggest standards to be tested for existence by the method of specimens. Here are some examples of the ways studies conducted by the method of relative frequencies can propose internal standards to be investigated further.

Gordon, Slade, and Schmitt (1986) reviewed a number of experiments in which student participants behaved differently from nonstudents. We should not conclude that all students have one kind of character and nonstudents some other kinds. After reviewing the kinds of tasks and judgments, however, on which students and nonstudents differ, one could ask oneself three kinds of questions: (1) How can we ascertain and describe some kinds of internal standards that some people of college age living in the academic setting have developed? (2) How do some people rearrange or recombine standards they had as college students to arrive at a new hierarchy of standards at later ages and in nonacademic settings? (3) Given a student and a nonstudent having similar internal standards, how do they use their different environments to maintain those similar standards?

A study that seems to me to plead for ideas about what many humans might be yearning for in the early years of their lives is one by Gottfredson (1981). He examined statistics on ages at which children were apprehended by police, and compared them with the local school-leaving age. His table 1 shows the numbers of boys per thousand, among 9,945 boys in Philadelphia born in 1945, who were first taken into custody by police at various ages. Beginning at seven years of age with fewer than five boys per thousand taken into custody for the first time, the number steadily increased with the age of the boys, even accelerated, and peaked at 16 years of age—the age at which the boys were legally permitted to leave school. The year after that, the numbers dropped precipitously. Among boys of low socioeconomic status, the number dropped from 117 per thousand at age 16 to 61 at age 17. Among boys of high socioeconomic status, the number dropped from 81 to 44.

What perceptions of their states of being were those apprehended boys trying to maintain by activities which, while they were in school, brought them into the arms of the police in ever-increasing numbers but which, after they could leave school, they could maintain in some other way? What perceptions took lower priority after they left school? And what about the boys who were never taken into custody? Did they have different purposes and yearnings, or did they have purposes and yearnings like those of the others but found ways of satisfying them in school that the others could not?

Gottfredson's sort of study does not pin down the internal standards; that would have to be done by the method of specimens. His study does not offer teachers or parents many ideas about what to do. But it does give clues to conditions that affect large proportions of individuals and is therefore useful in thinking both about how some young humans may function and about social policy.

Because I do not want this book to be a long one, I have not spent many pages on the usefulness of the method of relative frequencies. I hope, however, that I am leaving you in no doubt about my respect for the usefulness of the method in the conduct of human affairs.

SUMMARY

The method of relative frequencies is very good for casting nets. Pollsters, marketers, public health workers, and others make an honest living casting nets. The method is good for predicting situations in which certain proportions (relative frequencies) of people will be doing something to cope with something, though the method cannot tell you what any particular person will be doing nor what internal standard any particular person will be satisfying. It cannot even tell you (except by very risky inference) the internal standards that will be satisfied with relatively more frequency. I repeat, nevertheless, that the method is very good, as long as you stick to random samples, for estimating the incidence of auguries in further samples from the same population. Advertisers, politicians, and people who solicit contributions to causes will agree that casting a net is a good thing to be able to do.

The method is good for making catalogs and histories of people, conditions, and actions. It is good for getting hints of internal standards that people might be maintaining, giving you a good start on hunting for particular standards with more precision by using the method of specimens.

The method of relative frequencies is not good for finding out how humans function—neither how any particular person functions nor how humans as a species function. I will elaborate that claim in the rest of the book. Most psychologists do not study psychological invariants; they study statistics—that is, proportions of auguries. I am not, of course, saying that psychological invariants are the only sort of thing worth studying. The art of casting nets is worth studying, too.

3

Limitations to Sampling

The method of relative frequencies does not always require sampling. If you want to find out how many members of the office staff want to hold the annual picnic at Jones Beach, simply ask every one of them. If you want to know how many students can recognize an aspidistra, put one in the classroom and ask every student to write down its name. If you publish a newsletter and want to know how many of your subscribers care enough about telling you their opinions of your newsletter to return a brief questionnaire to you, send a copy of the questionnaire to all of them.

RANDOM SAMPLING

That last example easily raises the question of sampling. The cost of printing and postage to send the questionnaire to all subscribers might be more than you want to spend. In that case, you might settle for a sample. Usually, when we turn to samples, we do so to save both time and money. Often, we want to learn something about very large populations indeed. That is the reason the Census Bureau came into being and then, in this century, the national polling organizations with their highly sophisticated procedures for random sampling.

Often, time is as much a difficulty as money. You might want to interview people living in sparsely populated areas about their automobiles. But by the time you would drive hundreds or even thousands of miles to interview those scattered people, having to return several times to catch some of them or wait several hours for some of them to come home, some of the people you interviewed first would have bought new cars different from the cars you interviewed them about. If you wanted to come back to that population to do something with the information you got, you would be coming back to a changed population. In such a case, too, you might choose to interview only a fraction of the people so that you could complete your interviews more quickly.

The method of relative frequencies can work well—that is, give close estimates of the proportion in the population or in the next sample—only if it is used with a population of persons from which it is possible to sample randomly. The population must be listable, all members must be accessible for observing or querying, and the topic of investigation must be one in regard to which the characteristics of the respondents will change only insignificantly during the time it takes to collect the data. Your sample will lead you astray if by the time you have tallied up your results, the relevant characteristics of the population have changed. If you intend to check your estimate against another sample, the characteristics must change only insignificantly between the time you start the first sampling and end the second one.

Finally, the sample most be selected in such a way that every member of the population has an equal chance of getting into the sample. Ensuring every member's equal chance could be done by drawing slips of paper out of a hat; nowadays it is usually done by using a table of random numbers. Pollsters use several complex varieties of random sampling; area sampling, stratified sampling, and so on. With the special methods, the rule of an equal chance for every member is changed to read "a known chance." If, for example, the sample is drawn in such a way that people in Utah have twice the chance of getting into the sample that people in Ohio have, then your knowledge of that ratio enables you to apply the mathematics of probability just as well as if every potential member had the same chance. But those refinements never neglect the basic principles—that of random selection. My point here is simple, and to keep it simple I will use the term "random sampling" to mean any variety of sampling, simple or complex.

If you keep strictly to random selection of the people you want to study, you can do the things I described in Chapter 2: you can cast a net, catalog, write history, and hunt for hints of internal standards. Without random sampling, you can still hunt for hints of internal standards. Without random sampling, however, you cannot cast nets with any known accuracy, nor can you accurately catalog distributions of conditions and actions or trace histories of them.

Even with random sampling, the method of relative frequencies will not uncover for you the rules of functioning of the human creature, the nature of the beast. The method of relative frequencies can tell you how many people correspond to cells in a table or points on a graph that satisfy a specified relation. It can also tell you how closely the points approximate the relation. It cannot tell you whether the relation functions within a single particular person. It cannot enable you to understand better any single human nor, therefore, humans in general. I am presuming that the goal of understanding and predicting the way the human creature "works" is the cherished goal, at least the professed goal, of many academic researchers.

The next several chapters will offer arguments that the method of relative frequencies has been leading both workaday and formal researchers down the garden path and cannot do otherwise. Later, I will describe the method of specimens, a method as ancient as that of relative frequencies, and one which, like the method of relative frequencies, has had its own kind of signal successes. The method of specimens can demonstrate the maintenance of internal standards in single humans. But all that will come later. I return now to matters of sampling.

PRACTICAL DIFFICULTIES

Useful and profitable though it may be to cast a net with random sampling, it is not always easy to do. Sometimes it is impossible. Here is an example in which it is possible to conceive a population, but impossible, because of practical difficulties, to make a useful list of the population or to reach a random sample of it.

Suppose you want to study children of ages three through seven who are twins. Suppose you decide to study the population of twins of those ages in just one state of the United States forgoing the nation or the world. In Oregon, the counties collect information from hospitals about the births in them and from individuals who come to county offices to record births that occurred at home. After six months, counties send the information to the state. But some parents do not discover that they are required to register a birth until they take the child to school, and the registration is then five or six years late.

Furthermore, the information kept by the counties and the State of Oregon is in a certain way confidential. If you go in with the name of a person, you are allowed to look at the birth certificate of that person. But if you go in without a name, saying you want to find the names of all families to whom twins were born during a certain period, neither the county nor state office will let you do that. You might be reduced to poring over the vital statistics columns of all the newspapers in the state. Whether all newspapers would report late registrations, I do not know. Even if all did so, you would still miss some twins three or more years old who had not yet been registered. Maybe you know a quick and easy way out of those difficulties. I do not.

Then, by the time you had made your list, selected a random sample, and visited the families, some of the twins would have become older than seven years, other twins whose families you had not visited would have become three years old, and some of the children would have left the state. If you wanted to go back for more information, the population would have changed. Facing difficulties like those, it is no wonder that researchers who want to study twins rarely try to draw a random sample of some population of them.

Sampling Behavior Settings

I do not think we ever select a population or a sample to investigate without having in mind persons-in-situations. That is, we are not interested merely in enumerating people, but in counting proportions of them who do something or have some quality. Even the Census Bureau does more than count. Large survey organizations such as the Survey Research Center at the University of Michigan do define populations without having in mind any particular actions of their members, but they do that only because they are getting ready for the day when they *will* think of some possible actions of those people they will want to investigate. In brief, we define populations and draw samples not merely of people, but of persons-in-situations—that is, of interactions.

Sometimes researchers think in this form: "I want to study people who _____." Here are some examples:

are female.

are carpenters.

have cancer.

have an income below a certain amount per year.

are solving a puzzle.

are struggling to climb Mount Everest.

are dining at the Hoity-Toity Cafe.

are discussing politics.

In the first group of examples, the conditions are more-or-less stable characteristics of persons. We think of each example as a "subpopulation" of persons who _____. In the second group, the conditions are faced by persons only occasionally; persons do not carry them about as attributes. To sample people of the first sort, you can afford to take some time to find them; their attributes will still be with them—with most of them, at least—when you are ready to query or observe them. If you want, however, to sample randomly people "characterized" by activities like those in the second list, you will not have time to use the typical method used by the social surveyors. You will not have enough time, that is, to list all the people in a population, select a sample randomly, and then query them or observe them to find out whether they have the characteristics you care about.

To study people in now-and-then activity, you can select the people first; you can follow them around and note what they do when they engage in the activity. That can get very expensive. Or you can hang around a place where the activity is likely to occur, such as the Hoity-Toity Cafe or Mount Everest, and observe the people who come there. In that case, you cannot select the people randomly; they are selecting themselves.

It is reasonable, instead of studying people, to study the situations or conditions in which people act. That is, you can make a list of a population of colleges or restaurants or mountains, take a random sample of them, and study the human behavior that goes on there. You would be studying the behavior settings, treating the kinds of human behavior that are possible and impossible, frequent and rare, in those settings, as the characteristics of those settings.

Some behavior settings are easy to list as populations: all the fire stations in town, all the mountains in the world that have attracted at least ten climbers during the past five years, all the jobs in a company that have specified requirements and for which there were at least three applicants before someone was hired, or all the U.S. Army posts.

Some behavior settings or occasions for action, however, are impossible to list, be selected in a sample, and then observed. Examples: rebuffs to offers ("No, I would not like to join your committee"), spells of confusion in trying to solve a problem, misunderstandings in conversations, and so on. One difficulty with those occurrences is making the list in the first place; the occurrences do not have clear boundaries. Investigators will disagree on whether a particular rebuff is "strong" enough to count, whether a particular utterance is an offer, whether a confusion is long enough or muddled enough to be called one, and so on. The other difficulty with those occurrences is that they are evanescent. By the time you have counted the third instance, the first has vanished from your population. The difficulty is serious even with behavioral occasions that come and go much more slowly than the examples I have given. For example, Bullock and Svyantek (1987) have written a cogent article showing that it is impossible to use random strategies to study projects of organizational development.

Groups and Organizations

The method of relative frequencies requires researchers to choose a population and its members so that they have certain characteristics. First, every member must be recognizably bounded, so that we know when we have selected it or counted it. The member must not fade off indistinctly into its surroundings. Second, every member must maintain its characteristics at least for the time it takes to select and assess the first and second samples. If the population is changing, it must not change too fast for you to estimate the change by taking successive samples. Third, the population must be listable.

The method does not require homogeneity among the members of the population. The members can be as diverse as you wish; the mathematics of probability will still do its job. If you want to study persons with group membership as one of their characteristics, the diversity of members is no obstacle. That is little comfort, however, to researchers who want to use the method of relative frequencies to study groups as *things*, because most presumed members of the class of things we call human groups will fail to satisfy at least one of the three requirements I just listed.

In general, groups are not well bounded. They can overlap in membership. If you select a sample of 50 groups of ten members each, but groups *A* and *B* share three members between them, do you have 50 groups or 49.7 groups? The criterion of membership can also be indistinct. Should persons labeled honorary, emeritus, or associate be counted within the boundary of the group? Is a biological member of a family who lives a thousand miles away from the rest and hasn't written a letter in three years still within the boundary of the family group?

In general, groups do not have reasonably stable characteristics. Because of absences, the assortment of students in a classroom changes from day to day. The duties of a platoon in the Corps of Engineers will change from building a road this month to crowd control next month to keeping records in a warehouse the month after that. The group of people helping a candidate win an election will change in membership and assortments of duties at various stages and turns of fortune.

As to listing a population of groups, practical difficulties often make it impossible to do. Take four-member families. While you are selecting a sample, collecting data, and calculating your statistics, a lot of three-member families will enter your population (but not your data) by having produced a fourth member. A lot of families will leave your population (but not your data) through death or through the departure of a child who has grown old enough to leave home. As another example, take the population of groups demonstrating in protest of something. Think for a moment about the difficulties of knowing whether you should count some sort of group as a member of that population and whether a second researcher could replicate your study even a couple of months later.

Within the class of all conceivable groups, however, it is possible to find a few populations having well bounded members. The platoons in an army, it seems to me, are well and recognizably bounded—at least between changes in membership and if no one is on detached duty. It is also possible to find populations of groups that change members or other characteristics slowly enough so that they are substantially the same for the time it takes to list them and assess first and second samples: boards of directors of large firms, city councils between elections, monks and nuns in cloistered communities, athletic teams in the XYZ conference, and four-member families in which the wife is not pregnant and no child is more than twelve years old and you are taking samples small enough so that you can get your first and second samples within nine months.

It might even be possible to find populations of groups that satisfy all three criteria. The fraction of them will be small, however, among the kinds of groups sociologists and social psychologists like to study. It often happens that researchers want to investigate a topic for which finding a population of groups satisfying all three criteria is difficult or even impossible. The choices then are (1) to relinquish the group as a unit of analysis and study the behavior of individuals in those social settings, (2) to use a nonrandom sample, or (3) to use the method of possibilities.

The remarks I have made here about groups apply equally well to organizations. I think the difficulties I have listed occur even more often among organizations than among groups.

NONRANDOM SAMPLING

The mathematics of probability do not bend for researchers who have difficulties in listing a population or drawing a random sample. There is no evading the laws of chance. Must researchers, then, give up studying twins or industrial organizations? No, because more choices exist than that between random and nonrandom sampling. Researchers can choose the method of specimens or the method of possibilities. I will discuss those choices later in the book.

Much formal research and almost all everyday research using samples is done with nonrandom samples. The frequency, however, with which people rely on nonrandom samples is no more a testimonial to their reliability than the number of people who take pleasure in junk food is a testimonial to its nutrient value. Without random sampling, you have no way of estimating quantitatively the confidence you should put on the generalizability of your relative frequencies—that is, of estimating the probability that you will get the same proportion or pattern in your next sample.

The following justification for a nonrandom sample appeared in a widely respected journal: "Six thousand questionnaires were mailed, and [1,498] responses were received. . . . This response rate (25%) is consistent with response rates for other . . . surveys and typical of mail surveys generally." The argument seems to be that it must be all right to do things that way if other researchers do. If you want to discourage other researchers from pointing the finger of shame at you, that is a good argument. That kind of appeal to clemency from the reader appears frequently in professional research journals. If, however, you want to cast a net of calculable accuracy, that argument is irrelevant.

Randomly *assigning* persons to parts of an experiment who have been *selected* nonrandomly is no substitute for randomly selecting them from a listed population. When, with a nonrandom sample, you assign people randomly to experimental and control groups, you do equalize the chances (the chances, not the actual numbers) of people of some biased sort getting into one group or the other. That is helpful. But that unbiased assignment to the group, if you have selected the whole sample nonrandomly, helps you not one bit to estimate the probability that you will be able to replicate the results of the experiment.

Some people believe that more data are better than fewer data, even if the data come from nonrandom samples. That is the reasoning behind *meta-analy-*

sis, in which the results of many studies are assessed as from a single pool of data. Most of the studies assessed with meta-analysis have been done without random sampling, but if most of a hundred or more studies point in the same direction, we feel confident in investing some further effort in that direction. We will differ in our judgments of the odds we should give, but few of us will bet against the outcome of the meta-analysis. Despite our optimistic hope in collecting lots of data, however, a meta-analysis of nonrandom samples does not increase in any numerically specifiable degree our confidence in what the next sample will show. The numerical confidence levels issuing from meta-analyses are reliable only if all the constituent studies were of random samples. Nor does a meta-analysis of nonrandom samples enable us to describe or list a population that the constituent studies might have sampled.

I repeat: You cannot make a dependable numerical estimate of the probability of finding the results of your study replicated in the next sample (or, what is equivalent, estimate the likelihood that the population is changing) unless, both times, you select your samples randomly from the same listed population. That means that when you have conducted a study with a nonrandom sample and have written a statement about characteristics or behavior you think might be found among the people you hope are your population, you have no quantitative way of demonstrating to readers how much confidence they should have in your statements. You can only invite them to share your hope.

If academic psychologists (or economists, political scientists, sociologists, and so on) were always to draw their subjects from listable populations, the cat would be out of the bag. Researchers would discover that *any finding could be replicated* to a specifiable approximation a specifiable percentage of the time, *as long as the cross-validating studies* (second samples) *were made fast enough*, before too many people entered or left the population, before too many people changed their minds about things, and so on. Cronbach's complaint would soon become obvious to everyone:

> The trouble, as I see it, is that we cannot store up generalizations and constructs for ultimate assembly into a network. It is as if we needed a gross of dry cells to power an engine and could only make one a month. The energy would leak out of the first cells before we had half the battery completed. (1975, p. 123)

That is, researchers would give up trying to add more and more independent variables in the hope of predicting 98 percent of behavior on the Y variable, because, as they carried out replications and semi-replications in the "same" populations, they would discover that the populations they were sampling were changing their statistics (means, for example) faster than they could try new combinations of variables. They would then know that using the method of relative frequencies to find the conditions under which behavior can be predicted—that is, using more and more variables to slice the conditions into finer and finer slices—is a forlorn hope. I will say more about fine slicing in Chapter 7.

Cronbach is not the only one to worry. Here is an excerpt from a review by D. A. Phillips (1987) of a book containing eight chapters, all written by worriers:

> Baldwin and his colleagues call attention to the time-bound nature of developmental research and the knowledge it generates for parents, practitioners, and politicians. During the . . . time span of their . . . study of children at risk for schizophrenia, the diagnostic criteria for schizophrenia changed, prevalent family configurations changed, and theories about postpartum illness and family interaction changed. . . . What we can conclude, as well as what we ask and how we ask it, is hitched to social change and scientific advancement.
>
> This portrayal of psychology as infiltrated with social values, historical biases, and ideological predispositions could easily lead the reader to despair. (pp. 853-54)

Carrying out research with nonrandom samples can be fun. I have enjoyed it myself. Finding out whether the statistics come out the way you hoped is as suspenseful as finding out whether you will win a game of chess or cards or volleyball. But data from nonrandom samples will not enable you to cast a net of calculable reliability, not to speak of revealing the secrets of human nature.

THE JUNK BOX

To understand better the way sampling works, what it will tell you and what it will not, consider the analogy of a junk box. Suppose you have a big box of junk containing diverse objects such as corks, carburetors, and dead cockroaches. Let the junk in the box be your population of objects. The mathematics of probability is completely unaffected by the real things we let correspond to the numbers. The conclusions permitted by statistical inference are exactly the same whether you sample humans or junk.

You can draw samples of objects from the box and estimate the population statistics in the same way Gallup does with people. You can measure the maximum diameters of a sample of objects and estimate the mean maximum diameter in the population or the specific gravity, compressibility, height of bounce off a concrete floor, or market value. You can estimate changes in the population as you toss in more objects or remove some to be used in making repairs around the house. You can cast a net: if you select objects having a minimum diameter greater than three inches, you will catch a larger proportion of carburetor-like things than if you select objects smaller than that. You can hunt for correlations: the relation, for example, between maximum diameter and intensity of stink.

The parallel is obvious between a population of people and a population of

junk in estimating proportions in the population by taking a sample, in estimating changes in proportions or other statistics, and in casting the net. The
method of relative frequencies works well in both kinds of populations for
those purposes; you get reliable information of the kind you want.

It is obvious, too, that when you take a random sample of junk, measure the
diameters of the objects, and calculate the confidence you can have that the
mean diameter in the whole box lies within a certain distance of the sample
mean, you learn next to nothing about the character of the objects themselves—
about their weights or their shapes or whether they are capable of doing anything other than just sitting there. One object with a maximum diameter of six
inches could be a scrap of paper, another a half-rotten cantaloupe, and another
a priceless miniature painting.

You can get reliable estimates of correlations among the objects in the junk
box, too, but very often a reliable estimate is less than researchers want. Researchers are often hunting for *high* correlations. They are hunting for ways of
categorizing the junk so that if a thing lies in category *A* (or is high on variable
A), it will in 99 cases out of 100 lie also in category *B* (or be high on variable
B). I will use the analogy of the junk box to say more, therefore, about hunting
for correlations (or associations or contingencies) with the method of relative
frequencies.

Correlations

Let us suppose you have a hypothesis that things with moving parts must,
with rare exceptions, be composed of materials of a sufficient density. Here are
a carburetor, a baby's rattle, and a toy automobile, all made of rather dense
materials and all having moving parts. Over here are a block of softwood, a
sponge-rubber ball, and a chunk of styrofoam, all made of rather light materials
and all without moving parts. You take a random sample of junk to test whether
density of materials is correlated with possession of moving parts.

Just as in social science, you encounter some difficulties in measuring and
classifying. Suppose you measure density by submerging the object in a con-
tainer filled to the spout with water and noting the volume of water that spills
into a graduated beaker, then drying the object, then weighing it, and finally
dividing the weight by the volume of the spilled water. You have some difficulty with an aspirin tablet that half dissolves before you can get it dried off.
How can you always decide whether an object has moving parts? Are the pages
and covers of a book moving parts? The links of a chain? A button at the wrist
of a glove? Despite those perplexities, you make some decisions, as one always
must, and classify every object in your random sample according to density
and possession of moving parts. And, as often happens in social science too,
let us say that you get a moderate positive correlation.

Would your calculations of correlation describe for you any single piece of
the junk? Would your investigations tell you anything about the species *Junkus*

domesticus? I am not asking whether you would get statistics about the junk overall. Of course you would get statistics. I am asking whether you would discover any individual characteristic or any combination of characteristics that would enable you to identify an object as belonging to the species *Junkus domesticus* rather than to a species such as merchandise, garage-sale items, or heirlooms. My answer to those questions is *no*.

You might say you could examine individual objects to get some ideas about the nature of junk-objects—the kinds of materials needed for objects with moving parts and the kinds of materials that can compose objects without them. Certainly you could do that. But you would not do that by taking a random sample. You would hunt for pieces that would inspire you with insights. You wouldn't bother with a sample or a correlation. I will talk about the examination of specimens in Chapters 9 through 12.

Causal Experiments

You might think you could learn more about *Junkus domesticus* through the use of causal experiments. Suppose you have the hypothesis that objects of higher densities will be harder to compress than objects of lower densities. You draw a random sample of objects, put each one in turn on the table top and measure its height. Then you lower upon each object a ten-pound weight having a broad enough base to cover the object. You measure the height of the object again.

The carburetor squashes not at all. Nor does a block of hardwood, a brick, or a can of paint. The weight does compress to greater or lesser degrees, however, a pillow, a sponge-rubber ball, a scrap of balsa wood, and a dead cockroach. You get a statistically different degree of mean squashing between objects of high and low densities. You learn that denser things, on the average, squash less than less dense things.

You are now somewhat ahead of the game. You have put more meaning on the connection between (a) the relation of weight to volume and (b) susceptibility to squashing. That could give you some hints about what to study next about the characteristics of physical materials. That is analogous to getting some hints about kinds of internal standards some humans might be maintaining.

You may seek next to get more exact information, to reduce error, to achieve more precise predictions. You might, for example, choose to apply several different degrees of pressure. If you continue, however, to try to learn about characteristics of materials by the method of relative frequencies, you will encounter only frustration. In one sample, your averages will come from a mix of corks, carburetors, and cans of paint; in another, from a mix of books, chains, and gloves. The samples will continue to give different estimates. A few samples will be very different from the rest. Your estimates will cluster, but they will never agree within a range as small as the error of your physical measurements, and *your estimate of a population statistic will never be a description of any single piece of junk*. That is the nature of sampling.

By now, the two chief faults in this strategy for studying characteristics of materials are obvious. First, we should not be studying mixes of materials as if they were all instances of the same stuff. Second, our unit of analysis should not be the object, but the material. We ought to be studying natural kinds of materials such as wood, iron, plastic, styrofoam, brick, and paper, not cans, carburetors, books, pillows, and toy automobiles. If we are going to study materials, we will want to study one material at a time, and we will need only a few pieces of it. We will never think of selecting a random sample of pieces of iron.

Using the method of relative frequencies with the population of objects in the junk box, just as with some population of humans, can give us reliable estimates of statistics concerning the population and concerning further samples. Those statistics can have valuable practical uses. But the method of relative frequencies is powerless to tell us whether we are dealing with a species, a natural kind. It cannot even reliably separate living from nonliving things.

When we use sampling merely to estimate proportions of some characteristic in a population, as in simple polling, we are merely extrapolating. There is very little theory there. But when we use that strategy to try to discover how humans function as living creatures, the method requires us to act as if human individuals are only representative bearers of certain statistics characterizing a population, not as entities worthy of study in themselves as whole individuals. To the method of relative frequencies, a human is an exemplar of the species only in the way that a piece of junk is an exemplar of the collection in the junk box. That seems to me a strange conception of the human creature.

WHEN IT WORKS BEST

The method of relative frequencies, I believe, works best when almost everyone will agree that the entities sampled are clearly bounded and when they will agree upon the locations of the boundaries—the skins of humans, for example. It will work best, too, when the characteristics by which one intends to slice the population (or sample) are relatively long-lasting and readily observable by observer, interviewer, coder, and the like. Examples are whether the person lives in a house, apartment, or tent; whether the person is male or female; and the person's native language—though the last may be dubious in the case of persons very fluent in more than one language. The method works well but not quite as well with self-reports (using language) of long-lasting characteristics that are easily verified such as number of children, number of automobiles owned, and whether the person is employed. It works least well (though still well enough for some purposes) with self-reports of changeable inner states such as beliefs, opinions, attitudes, and so on.

SUMMARY

Studying nonrandom samples is somewhat useful for getting hints about internal standards. It is no good for casting nets or making representative catalogs. Random sampling is very effective for all those purposes. If, however, researchers were to insist upon random samples, they would become much less confident that the method of relative frequencies can uncover the characteristic functioning of the species *Homo sapiens sapiens*.

Taking statistics from a sample delivers estimates of statistics in the population. It does not deliver knowledge about the functioning of any one individual in the sample or population.

Great practical difficulties arise in trying to take samples of some kinds of populations. Indeed, one can conceive some populations that seem impossible to sample randomly. Given the limits on what the method of relative frequencies can tell us even when we sample randomly, and given the difficulties and even sometimes the impossibility of random sampling, it is obvious that the method of relative frequencies cannot bring us all the kinds of information we want to get from research.

II

What the Method of Relative Frequencies Will Not Do

In Part I, I asserted that the method of relative frequencies was incapable of delivering the secrets of human nature—the manner in which the species, as a species, functions. In Part II, I will display several features of the method any one of which deprives it of that capability. I will display the features in connection with various sub-activities in social-science research: conducting experiments, interpreting correlations, using words with "subjects" (the people studied) and colleagues, and fine slicing, the latter being my name for what is nowadays called "contingency theory."

The method of relative frequencies is a metatheory. That is, it requires researchers to act as if they are making certain assumptions about human behavior. The chapters in Part II will pay a good deal of attention to these assumptions. I will show how researchers customarily use those assumptions to replace actual data. The point is the same as that made by E. F. Schumacher in the quotation that appears in the front of this book. The attention to assumptions will continue in Parts III and IV (see also "assumptions" in the index). In Part III, I will show how the linear or straight-line metatheory of causation underlying current uses of the method of relative frequencies also vitiates the method. There I will also argue that the circular metatheory is more suitable.

4

Experiments

I do not claim that very many of the ideas in this book are original with me. I hope only that I have brought together some good ideas so that their connection gives them fresh force. What I will call here the substitution of persons, for example, has worried many psychologists for a good many decades. Some psychologists have touched on it when discussing the nomothetic strategy versus the idiographic—that is, the strategy of studying differences among people in the same situation versus studying differences in the behavior of a single person across different situations. As long ago as 1974, Bem and Allen gave a good account of the arguments and the discomfiture. Good recent examples are the chapters by Franck and by Grossman in 1986.

The method of relative frequencies deals with statistics about anonymous people. It does not reveal who falls into some cell in a contingency table, but only how many. It does not reveal who gets a particular pair of scores on X and Y, but only how many people show similar ratios of X to Y. It does not reveal who gets a score above or below a mean, but only whether enough people have high enough scores to bring the mean to a point higher than some other mean. The method of relative frequencies never deals with any one person pursuing an individual purpose, but only with statistics (means, correlations, and so on) about abstracted aspects of behavior tallied over a collection of people.

Treating people as anonymous and interchangeable units works very well in casting nets, making catalogs, and writing histories. The strategy is entirely suitable to those purposes, since the only logic necessary is that of extrapolating statistics. When we try, however, to learn about the nature of the human from correlations and causal experiments, the method requires a string of shaky assumptions.

EXAMPLE

I sometimes peruse reports of research on the self-concept. I will give here an account of one I happened upon and use it to exhibit the difficulties we must inevitably encounter when we use the method of relative frequencies in the search for the inner nature of humans. I am deeply grateful to Drs. Dieter Frey and Dagmar Stahlberg for their permission to discuss their work (1986) in this way.

Frey and Stahlberg gave an intelligence test to about 80 high school students. Then they told those subjects to write down the score they expected to get on the test. Six days later, the experimenters gave folders to all the subjects containing their purported scores. The purported scores, however, were all 18 points below the scores the subjects said earlier they expected to get. The folders repeated for the subjects the estimates they had written six days earlier of the scores they would get.

The experimenters did that because they wanted to threaten the subjects' self-esteem. They assumed that getting a score on an intelligence test 18 points lower than expected would cause the subjects to worry about maintaining a picture of themselves they preferred. But I have not said that quite right. The experimenters themselves, I am sure, were not as naive as to expect that *all* the subjects would worry. What I mean here and throughout these chapters is not that every experimenter either consciously or unconsciously makes the assumptions I am writing about, but that the very use of the method of relative frequencies requires researchers to *act as if* they are making the assumptions. In conducting this study of self-concept, the experimenters had to *act as if* all the subjects would worry. And when they acted like that, the experimenters then had to accept still other assumptions: (1) that all the subjects were hearing and reading accurately the instructions and information the experimenters gave them (for example, when I talk to an audience or pass out written instructions, one listener or reader among three or four dozen takes a meaning exactly the opposite of what I try to convey, no matter how plainly I think I have said it or written it, no matter whether I repeat it three times, no matter how large the type on the page, and others misunderstand less dramatically, but to some large or small degree); and (2) that all the subjects included intelligence in the sense of a score on a test pushed at them by persons in authority (not a test they had chosen to take on their own initiative) in the self-concept they wanted to protect. As much research shows and as we are often reminded in our daily lives, most people most of the time in our culture—perhaps especially students when sitting in a classroom—do try to maintain a good opinion of their intelligence. I say here only that people vary a good deal in the importance they give to it and in the way they conceive it. The experimenters did not report, for example, any sweating, trembling, or cries of anguish.

Adolescents are accustomed to conforming, at least superficially, to what their teachers and visiting experts tell them to do. Some of them get swept up in what they are told to do and adopt it as something they want to do; some do not. I have no way of estimating, from the information given in the article, what portion of the subjects were worried when they saw their purported scores. Subjects for whom those assumptions did not hold would not be worrying about their self-concepts. It is reasonable to suppose that there were at that point two classes of subjects:

Y. Those who were worrying about their self-concepts.

N. Those who were not.

Actually, there were no doubt degrees of worrying, but to make things simpler here, I will divide all those possible degrees of worrying into just two classes: "*Y*" for yes and "*N*" for no. The experimenters proceeded as if all subjects were in the class "*Y*".

The experimenters next divided the subjects randomly in half. They gave one group two short articles about intelligence tests to read, telling them the articles had been written by experts. The articles disparaged intelligence tests, saying that the tests were incapable of measuring intelligence. The other group got no articles to read.

The experimenters did that to cause subjects in the first group to worry less about their self-concepts than those in the second group. Their reasoning was that subjects in the first group could say to themselves something like, "The experts who wrote these articles are telling me that my low score is probably not the truth about me, anyway." Here the experimenters must accept the assumption that they were right; that is, (1) that all the subjects in the first group read the messages and the articles with sufficient understanding, and (2) that their understanding did indeed reduce their anxiety.

If research by the method of relative frequencies has taught us anything in all these years, surely it is that people differ. It is likely that some subject among those 80 was wholly unstirred throughout the experiment. It is also likely that some subject was terrified at the sight of the test score 18 points lower than expected.

It is possible that some of those who felt the *greatest* anxiety over their reported test scores were *least* able to use the information as a path to reducing their anxiety. A lot of research has shown that under strong emotional arousal, people often give poor attention to certain information in their environments. I have not myself conducted deceptive experiments, but I remember a colleague telling me that he once spent two hours trying to convince a subject that a score the subject had received on a purported test (which was actually a test of nothing) did not and could not disqualify him from becoming an officer in the army.

But the subject had become so distraught that he simply could not understand what my colleague was saying and went away disconsolate. It is possible, therefore, that some of those who received the test-disparaging information did not reduce their anxiety.

Among those in the test-disparaging group who did not get anxious despite the discrepancy between expected and reported score, probably most would remain unanxious, but some, after receiving more information, might begin to wonder whether there might, after all, be something to worry about. Perhaps they would pick up some clues from the anxious subjects in the room. Those sequences of behavior seem to me less likely than those the experimenters hypothesized, but, as I said earlier, people do differ in their behavior.

Then there were those in the no-disparagement group. The experimenters hoped those subjects would have been anxious about their self-concepts and would have remained that way. No doubt that was the case for some, even most. For one reason or another, however, some subjects may not have fitted that pattern. Some might have become less anxious because they found their own defenses of their self-concepts without having to be given one by the experimenters (it is a frequent assumption of researchers devoted to linear causation that people do nothing until prodded or enticed by an experimenter). Some, like some in the other group, might have cared so little about the experiment that they did not become anxious in the first place. Some of those might have become anxious later, some not.

I don't want you to think that I believe the experimenters were unthinking dolts. While they were designing their experiment, they surely thought about all the ways their hopes could be frustrated. Indeed, their report touches on a good many of the troubles I am pointing out here. My point is not that most experimenters are simpletons, but that the *method of relative frequencies requires experimenters to act as if they are unaware* of the ways humans can slip under the fences erected by experimental designs. Even though the experimenters know that some of their subjects are not going to behave as predicted, the method requires the experimenters to act as if those subjects do behave as predicted.

All told, there were eight possibilities, four in the test-disparaging group and four in the no-disparagement group. The designations "*Y*" and "*N*" below do not indicate whether the subject was worried. The "*Y*" means the result the experimenters wanted to happen, the "*N*" the result they did not.

In the no-disparagement (*ND*) group:

(*ND*)-*Y.Y.* Those who, after seeing their unexpectedly low scores, started worrying and were still worrying.

(*ND*)-*N.Y.* Those who had not worried at seeing their scores but started to worry
later.

(*ND*)-*Y.N.* Those who had been worrying but later worried less or not at all.

(*ND*)-*N.N.* Those who had not worried at first and were still not worrying.

In the test-disparaging (*TD*) group:

(*TD*)-*Y.Y.* Those who had been worrying about their self-concepts and who were now worrying less than they had been.

(*TD*)-*N.Y.* Those who had not worried at first and were still not worrying.

(*TD*)-*Y.N.* Those who had been worrying about their self-concepts and who were still worrying as much as ever (or possibly even more).

(*TD*)-*N.N.* Those who had not worried at first but started to worry after they read the test-disparaging information.

Next, the experimenters told all the subjects that a lot of controversy was going on about the effectiveness of intelligence tests, and they passed out to the subjects in both groups copies of a list of ten fictitious articles, saying that the subjects "might be interested in reading more." Annotations in the list made it clear (to those subjects who read the annotations and did so with adequate comprehension) that five of the articles argued in favor of the validity of intelligence testing, and five against. Subjects were then instructed to mark on 7-point scales how "interested" they were in reading each article.

Now, of course, the experimenters were predicting that the subjects in the no-disparagement group would want to read more articles disparaging intelligence tests than articles supporting their use. They were predicting, too, that the subjects in the test-disparaging group, who had already read disparaging remarks presumably written by experts, would have little preference between the test-disparaging and test-supporting articles. As it turned out, most of the subjects did indeed fall into that predicted pattern; the results were statistically significant.

Now some further assumptions enter. Here are two I think important: (1) that if the subjects in the test-disparaging group had been in the no-disparagement group, they would have acted as those in that group did, and vice versa—that subjects in the two groups were substitutable for one another. This assumption is implicit whenever experimenters assign subjects randomly to two or more groups. And (2) that within either group, subjects were substitutable for one another in regard to their scores on preference for reading one kind of article or the other listed on the handout.

The subjects' reading of the list of ten articles gives us two new categories: those who chose articles in conformity with the hypothesis and those who chose them contrary to the hypothesis. Multiplying those two by the eight I listed earlier gives us 16 categories, including as examples:

(*ND*)-*Y.Y.Y.* Those who were worried when they saw the score that was lower than expected, who remained worried, and who chose articles according to the prediction for the ND group.

(*ND*)-*Y.Y.N.* Those who were worried by the reported score, who remained worried, but who chose articles *contrary* to prediction.

(TD)-N.N.Y. Those who had not worried at first, but started to worry after they read the test-disparaging information, but who nevertheless chose articles according to the prediction for the TD group.

(TD)-N.N.N. Those who had not worried at first, but started to worry after reading the test-disparaging information, and who chose articles *contrary* to prediction.

Among the 16, the only sequences of behavior that would have satisfied the experimenters fully are those in which everything went according to prediction, namely:

(ND)-Y.Y.Y. Those who were worried when they saw the score that was lower than they expected, who remained worried while members of the other group were reading their test-disparaging handouts, and who, when given the list of possible articles to read, rated the test-disparaging articles as considerably more attractive, on the average, than the test-supporting articles.

(TD)-Y.Y.Y. Those who were worried when they saw the score that was lower than they expected, who became less worried as a result of reading the test-disparaging information handed to them, and who, when given the list of possible articles to read, rated the attractiveness of the two kinds of articles, on the average, about equally.

Those two categories, however, did not contain all the subjects whose choice of articles the experimenters counted as favorable to the hypothesis. When they carried out their statistical analyses, they perforce also counted as favorable the choices made by subjects in all other categories ending in "*Y*," namely:

(ND)-N.Y.Y.	*(TD)-N.Y.Y.*
(ND)-Y.N.Y.	*(TD)-Y.N.Y.*
(ND)-N.N.Y.	*(TD)-N.N.Y.*

According to the experimenters' theory, those subjects should not have rated the attractiveness of the articles as they did. Nevertheless, the experimenters counted the ratings given by those subjects as supporting their hypothesis. That is standard practice, too.

The remaining eight cartegories are these:

(ND)-Y.Y.N.	*(TD)-Y.Y.N.*
(ND)-N.Y.N.	*(TD)-N.Y.N.*
(ND)-Y.N.N.	*(TD)-Y.N.N.*
(ND)-N.N.N.	*(TD)-N.N.N.*

Some mysteries hide here, too. Consider for a moment the subjects in the category *(ND)-Y.N.N.* They were worried at first, then less so (perhaps some of them not at all), and then showed no preference for disparaging articles over the nondisparaging. That is exactly the behavioral sequence of the subjects I classified as *(TD)-Y.Y.Y.* Think of that! Should the subjects showing the *(ND)- Y.N.N.* sequence have been counted as supporting the hypothesis? I do not know.

Why did the experimenters count those various categories of subjects the way they did? They did it because they did not know who was in those categories. They did not know which subjects were unworried by the discrepant scores they were shown. They did not know which subjects in the *TD* group failed to be reassured by the disparaging information from the fictitious experts.

Experimenters do often try to find out whether subjects are responding the way they hope to the "treatment" or "induction." For example, after showing the subjects their purported scores, these experimenters might have asked the subjects whether they were worried about their self-concepts. In this case, querying the subjects might or might not have "purified" the sample of subjects. Some might have denied worrying even though they actually were worrying, and some might have said they were worrying when they actually were not.

With the *TD* group, after showing the subjects the disparaging passages to read, the experimenters might have asked the subjects a second time whether they were worried. The same uncertainties would have arisen. Furthermore, after having been asked twice whether they were worried, some of the subjects in the *TD* group would surely have thought, "Oh, the experimenters are trying to make us worry about our intelligence," or the contrary, "trying to keep us from worrying." Either way, the opinion would probably have some effect on the ratings of the articles—an effect the experimenters did not want. Furthermore, the *ND* group would have been asked the question about worrying once, and the *TD* group twice. That would make an imbalance between the two groups that the experimenters also would not want. The method of relative frequencies always encounters difficulties of this sort.

At no step did the experimenters know how many subjects fell into one category or another. We end with sixteen categories (more, if you want to think about finer degrees of worrying and rating the articles) that might have contained subjects and probably did. The experimenters hoped that the great bulk of the favorable responses to the list of articles came from subjects who actually went through the sequences of behavior *(ND)-Y.Y.Y.* and *(TD)-Y.Y.Y.* But it is possible that a large number of the favorable responses, even a majority (we have no evidence to the contrary) came from the other six categories ending in *"Y."*

If we are accustomed to putting confidence in research done by the method of relative frequencies when a computation of an inferential statistic delivers a "significant" value, it is very easy for us to believe that the bulk of the subjects must have behaved as the hypothesis specified. In this case, it is tempting to believe that the bulk of the subjects must have behaved in the patterns (*ND*)-*Y.Y.Y.* and (*TD*)-*Y.Y.Y.* Yet three point are inescapable.

First, the significance test tells us only the probability that the two arrays of final scores could have occurred from having been drawn randomly from a common pool. It tells us nothing, not even by inference, about what happened to the subjects earlier in the experiment, previous to the final measurement.

Second, we have no direct evidence to tell us how many subjects were actually behaving in any one of the 16 patterns. We would like to believe that the numbers of people in the patterns contrary to hypothesis were small, but we have no way of estimating those numbers. The success of the experiment was calculated on the fall of scores that could have come from any of the eight patterns ending in *Y*. We have no way of knowing how many scores came from the two of those eight patterns that conformed fully to the hypothesis. If we could have known the subjects who showed the 16 patterns and could have sorted them by pattern instead of by assigned group, the final result might have been more favorable or less favorable to the experimenters' hypothesis; there is no way we can know. Certainly one thing is clear. *The experiment gives us no data that enable us to point at any one subject and say, "That subject behaved according to hypothesis."* We would like to think some did, but we have no way of knowing how many did or who they were.

Third, though the experimenters did not say so explicitly, presumably they would like us to think that any person encountering a threat to self-concept would behave in a manner similar to their prediction for the *TD* group, and that the same person acting without such a threat would behave in a manner similar to their prediction for the *ND* group. But they did not put any subject into both situations. It seems to me that most psychologists, and certainly most readers of the popular psychology press, would like to use data such as came from this experiment to say something like, "When our self-concept is threatened, we_____and when it is not, we_____" meaning that any one of us can behave *both* ways. But the experimenters gave us no data to show that a person could behave in both ways.

Overall, isn't this a strange story? Here, as in almost all its applications to the study of the dependence of behavior on environmental events, the method of relative frequencies wants us to believe, so to speak, that it has told us how a lot of people have behaved, even though, by its very procedure, *it fails to demonstrate that any single person has actually behaved that way.*

The experimenters concluded, "The devaluation of the importance of intelligence in the serious ego-threat [ND] condition seems to be a clear indicator of motivational drives to protect self-esteem." But the experimenters did not observe actual devaluation in the sense of a person evaluating something lower than before. The experimenters based their conclusion on the fact that on the average some people made lower evaluations than *others*. And among the scores that went to make up the averages, some people in the group with the lower average actually gave scores that were *higher* than some of the scores in the group with the higher average, and conversely. To reach their conclusion, in sum, the experimenters substituted the scores of people in one group for the scores they thought people in the other group would have gotten had they observed them in the first group's condition, and they said that subjects in one group devalued intelligence in comparison to the other group even though the fact was that some individuals in the one group did *not* do so in comparison to some individuals in the other group, thus substituting in a certain strange way low scores for high and vice versa.

I want to say again that I did not pick this study as a "bad" example. I did not pick it to exhibit unusually strange assumptions. I use it here because it seems to be a typical application of the method of relative frequencies and because it shows clearly the core assumptions required in a typical use of that method. The assumptions are not necessarily assumptions that experimenters like; they are assumptions the method foists upon us.

Now I will briefly describe the substitution of people in more general terms. Social scientists often observe a person in condition *A* (such as encountering a threat) showing behavior high on variable *X* and *another* person in condition *B* (such as not encountering a threat) showing behavior low on *X*. The researchers then often assume without test that *both* of those particular persons would show high *X* in condition *A* and low *X* in condition *B* if both had been subjected to both conditions. Observing different people in different conditions is taken as equivalent to observing the same person in different conditions as below:

```
Condition A          Condition B
--------------       --------------
Mary showing         Maud showing         (Different persons in
high X in A          low X in B           different conditions)

can substitute       can substitute
for (is inter-       for (is inter-
changeable with)     changeable with)

either Mary or       either Mary or       (Same persons in
Maud showing         Maud showing         the different
high X in A          low X in B           conditions)
```

When we generalize to Mona, who was not in the experiment at all, we must make these assumptions.

```
Condition A          Condition B
--------------       --------------
Mary showing         Maud showing         (Different observed
high X in A          low X in B           persons)

can substitute       can substitute
for (is inter-       for (is inter-
changeable with)     changeable with)

Mona showing         Mona showing         (Same unobserved
high X in A          low X in B           person)
```

Therefore, despite our having observed Mary and Maud in the different conditions, not Mona, the assumption is that Mona would behave like Mary in condition *A* and like Maud in condition *B*. The method of relative frequencies requires that kind of assumption whenever researchers put subjects in experimental and control groups and when they write about some unspecified people beyond the experiment.

CODA

If your purpose is that of casting a net, the assumptions I have described cause no embarrassment. You will maintain random selection in successive samples, and you wish only to predict the proportions of people who will show particular combinations of values on variables (high on this, low on that), and you are prepared to accept a specifiable degree of error in your prediction. You do not actually care whether people are alike or different. You are simply extrapolating from sample to population and are able to anticipate ranges of error in your estimates regardless of the sources of the errors. It is useful to be able to make an estimate of how many Democrats will vote for the Democratic candidate, regardless of whether you have any idea about the causes of the concatenation.

The method of relative frequencies requires you to assume that all humans function alike (are interchangeable one for another), but it can never test that assumption, because it can tell you nothing about any single human. (The method of specimens, too, begins with the assumption that all humans function alike, but it can test the assumption, as I will show in later chapters.) If you want to learn something about the internal functioning of the human animal, the method of relative frequencies will not teach you.

Nevertheless, many researchers undertake to give advice about what behavior to expect from Mona. On the basis of research conducted, for example, in a psychological laboratory with samples of subjects of a narrow age range who grew up when our culture had a particular cast and in which subjects showed higher *X* in condition *A* only on the average than did those in condition *B*, many researchers, professors, counselors, teachers, clergy, writers of psychological articles for popular magazines, and parents announce that anybody (any particular individual person) in any situation that includes condition *A* will show high *X*. Regardless of whether the samples of subjects are random or nonrandom, that kind of generalization is sheer folly.

You might be saying, "Well, everybody knows that there are slips and inaccuracies and unreliabilities in research. But it all comes out in the wash. That's the point of randomizing and replication and accumulating evidence and the free market of ideas and all that." Well, no matter how many rags you wash, they don't turn into a tuxedo. I hope I have shown in this chapter (and again in the next) that the accumulated "evidence" from the method of relative frequencies is actually an accumulation of very dubious assumptions.

Many researchers nowadays hope that meta-analysis (analyzing statistically the statistics from many studies) will point us to the truth. For me, however, the chief virtue of meta-analysis is that it shows so clearly in one domain of research after another the watery soup that the method of relative frequencies has delivered to us.

After having seen only *some* subjects behave in a certain way (albeit a statistically significant number), many researchers seem willing to declare that they now know something about all people. They may not actually write "all" people or subjects, but when they omit to write "some," I can suppose only that they mean anybody or everybody. Such sentences are not rare. They occur regularly in the professional journals and books. Here are a few among the thousands you can find for yourself in any library:

> adults who have been successful at a task, and hence momentarily self-accepting, are more willing to give money to a confederate of the experimenter's than those who have not been successful and thus more concerned about their own self-acceptance.

Are *all* adults who have been successful, every one, more willing than any who have not been successful? I doubt it.

> Several studies have shown that an individual's belief and attitude statements can be manipulated by inducing him to role-play, deliver a persuasive communication, or engage in any behavior that would characteristically imply his endorsement of a particular set of beliefs.

Did the studies show that *every* individual was successfully manipulated in all those ways? I would not complain if the author had written ". . . can *sometimes* be manipulated. . . ."

Here is a prize example from an article about the working conditions of teachers:

> A finding worthy of note is that teachers seem to have constant problems with the quantity of assistance from teacher aides. Over 12 percent of all respondents . . . fall into this category.

Those two sentences seem to me contradictory. Do teachers have constant problems about aides? Well, about 12 percent of them do. Twelve percent seems to me very different from the unqualified "teachers."

Writing about variables instead of people also implies that everybody showed the behavior:

> [The authors] exposed pictures with approximately this same degree of blurredness for four seconds each in an EEG experiment and found them to evoke longer-lasting desynchronization than clear versions of the same pictures.

Did every person show longer-lasting desynchronization with blurred than with clear pictures? Possibly so, but that is quoted from a review of many studies, and data were not given. Because of the way many social scientists write, I cannot be sure whether every person showed the effect.

> Information inputs are more effective in bringing about arousal (and commanding attention) if they are, among other things, intense; spatially extensive; moving; changing; novel; heterogeneous; repeated a few times; contrasting in color, pattern, or in other ways; or complex, i.e., high in information content.

Do those information inputs always, with every subject under any condition, bring about "more effective . . . arousal"? The method of relative frequencies cannot justify statements like those above. The method permits us to say that *some* people have been observed to behave in such-and-such a manner and even that the distribution of our observations between groups would be unlikely to occur only by chance. The method does not, however, permit us the kind of blanket statement I have illustrated. I think Valsiner (1986) agrees with me about this.

One of my colleagues proposed to me the possibility that most researchers are aware when they write "the subjects" that they mean some, not all of them, but use "the subjects" as shorthand instead of writing out "some subjects" or "most of the subjects." I cannot believe it. First, the extra words are so few that shorthand is not needed. And second, I would certainly expect, if researchers were actually using shorthand, that introductory texts would explain the shorthand to beginning students. But I have never seen such an explanation.

For the research community at large, a vital phase of any research is the research report. For all of us who were not present during the conduct of the study, the researcher's words and numbers are all we have to go by. It seems to me that writers of research reports should take meticulous, even excruciating, care in telling what happened and what we might reasonably expect to happen elsewhere. Doing so would at least make it harder for us to fool ourselves.

SUMMARY

The method of relative frequencies requires us to act as if people are substitutable for one another, are interchangeable—that they will behave alike except for (1) the effects of the independent and intervening variables the researcher wants to study and (2) the random variability inherent in every particular individual. Furthermore, it requires us to act as if all subjects *within* experimental groups act in the ways called for by the experimental design, even though most experimenters know that cannot be the case.

The method of relative frequencies requires us to conclude that the people in an experimental group, or at least a statistically significant number of them, have behaved in a certain way, even though, by its very procedures, the method usually fails to demonstrate that any single person has actually behaved that way.

Though the fact in almost every study in social science is that only *some* subjects act as the experimenters predict, nevertheless many researchers (not only the popular writers) talk and write as if *all* the subjects act as expected. This misleads everyone—public, students, and the researchers themselves.

The method of relative frequencies requires us to take it on faith that the humans in our investigations are interchangeable; the method itself is incapable of testing that assumption. In the next chapter, I will show how that faith underlies some further research techniques. In Part IV of the book, I will show how the method of specimens enables us to test the assumption.

5

Correlations

Since the method of relative frequencies always deals with *numbers* of people—and with distributions and averages of them—the assumption of the substitutability of persons (''subjects'') runs through every submethod and technique of analysis. It permeates the use of correlations in a very strange way.

Within the method of relative frequencies, we almost always think of a relation as a two-way distribution of people or other entities. We can portray the idea most simply with a four-celled contingency table. Each cell contains the number of people whose categories are those heading the row and column:

		Y	
		Democrats	Republicans
	Easterners	40	55
X			
	Westerners	60	35

All other relations are elaborations of that basic pattern—tables with more than two rows or columns, tables with more than two variables for categorizing, and even the several varieties of bivariate and multivariate correlation, in

Figure 5.1
Typical Scatter-plot of a Correlation

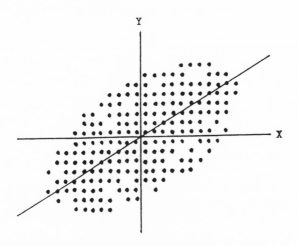

which many, even all, of the "cells" contain only one person. For convenience here, I will call all those distributions "correlations."

Researchers want to make a simple statement that will summarize somehow all the pairs of scores in a correlation. You could simply look at the scatter-plot. The plot might be fairly well formed, as in Figure 5.1, but scatter-plots are often more irregular than that one. Judging scatter-plots by eye to compare them would be more an artistic endeavor than a quantitative one. Social scientists like to use numbers whenever possible. Furthermore, social scientists like to make predictions. From merely looking at a scatter-plot, it is difficult to make a simple statement about the way X predicts Y. It is true that if you pick one particular value of X, you can see from the scatter-plot that you should predict some value of Y lying between the bottom and the top of the scatter on the vertical line defined by the value of X. But what can you say in general, no matter what the value of X, about the way the values of X narrow the possible locations of Y?

That question demands some scheme for putting a number on the shape of the scatter-plot. Hence the fondness for correlation coefficients. That single number, the correlation coefficient, gives you a measure of the amount of uncertainty you can remove from your guessing about Y, if you were to make a lot of guesses, by knowing the value of X beforehand.

PREDICTION AND ERROR

If you want to cast a net, if you want to capture as successfully as possible persons who have a certain value on Y (such as the amount of money spent for the current family automobile) by using values of X (such as an index of socioeconomic status), then you want to have a number that will tell you, overall, how good your net is—how well you can predict Y from X. That is the problem that Francis Galton and Karl Pearson solved for us so nicely 80 and more years ago. But the problem they solved was that of predicting statistical association, not that of explaining behavior. Correlations taken over an array of people can tell us nothing about what goes on in any single person.

The conception of error in casting a net is very different from the conception of error in hunting for a "true" or "underlying" relation. In casting a net, you simply want to know how close you can come in finding something labeled Y_j if you note that it is labeled X_i. You don't have to assume that Y was caused by X or vice versa or that any particular Y_j is any more "true" or "real" or "uninfluenced by uncontrolled variables" than any other. But a correlation coefficient is a coefficient in a linear equation that delivers to you, for any one value of X, one and only one value of Y, and many people believe that there must be a function inside humans (or a significant number of them) that mirrors that one-to-one relation. Unfortunately, a correlation taken over a collection of people has nothing to say on that matter.

For example, the linear correlation between the height and weight of human bodies is rather strong. But it makes no sense to say that there is an "underlying" relation on which there will somehow be a single value of Y for any single value of X, and people who weigh more or less than the average at that height are somehow in "error." You can say that people too far from the average weight will be in peril of illness of some sort, but that has nothing to do with whether we are having difficulty with errors that interfere with our search for the "true" relation. You certainly cannot say that people "tend" toward the regression line (the diagonal line in Figure 5.1). The person who is too fat is as likely to be "tending" toward getting fatter as toward getting thinner. A correlation, no matter how strong, does not imply that the causal connections would show us a one-to-one relation if only we could get rid of the error. Mace and Kratochwill (1986, pp. 155-57) make much the same point in a different way.

My point is that with many of the correlations that social scientists calculate, they have only a hope, a hypothesis, and no evidence whatever, that an error-free scatter of points would fall into a one-to-one relation (like the regression line in Figure 5.1) nor, if it did, that the relation would be the regression line. The actual relation might be like that of height and weight in animals.

Uncertainty in being able to predict is not the same thing as error in measurement. For example, the number of seats in a vehicle is related to the number of people you will observe riding in it. The relation looks like this:

```
Riders

  5                       x

  4                   x   x

  3               x   x   x

  2           x   x   x   x

  1       x   x   x   x   x

          1   2   3   4   5  .  .  .
```

Seats

The number of seats has a direct effect on the number of riders. A vehicle with 20 seats, for example, will be observed to be carrying any number of persons from zero to 20 (not counting the driver and assuming that people are not permitted to stand in the aisle) but not more than 20. You could calculate the correlation between seats and riders. You would get a moderate positive correlation. But it would be silly to argue that the regression line represents the "true" or "actual" relation between seats and riders, or that somehow riders were "tending" to appear in certain numbers, or that numbers of riders other than those on the regression line were somehow erroneous. There would certainly be very little error in measurement. Anyone who knows the integers can count, with high reliability, the numbers of seats and riders.

But social scientists often want to use correlations to try to find lawful relations between variables, to find necessary connections. They know, of course, that a correlation cannot tell us whether the cause goes from X to Y or vice versa or from some unmeasured variable Z to both X and Y. But having taken measures of X and Y from a collection of persons, and having found a pattern that would be unlikely by sheer chance, social scientists then almost always assume that *something* causal is going on.

The assumption that an array of data exhibiting regularities of some sort betrays some natural necessity at work, some lawfulness beyond a mere chance occurrence, underlies all scientific work. But when we are dealing with living creatures, the assumption that every point in a scatter-plot got there because of the variables the researcher chose to measure goes beyond that first necessary assumption. It also requires the assumptions that (1) the two variables are dealt with in the same way within every person and (2) the deviations from the regression line are aberrations or "error."

In the social sciences, we collect a cloud of points and then proclaim that the line from which the points have the least mean squared deviation must be the one we are hunting for. Not only that, we almost always proclaim that the line we are hunting for must necessarily be straight. If the points turn out to be less scattered than chance would leave them, we seem ready to believe that all those points were trying, so to speak, to array themselves on a straight line but were somehow buffeted or confused by "error." Social scientists use the term "error" to mean any deviation of data from where they hoped the data would fall, regardless of whether the deviation is due to imprecisions of measurement or to effects of unmeasured variables. Most write as if the buffeting and confusion is always going on, and that it always occurs in such a way as to produce a cloud of minimum mean squared deviation from where the data-points really wanted to be, so to speak. I will show another manifestation of this mistake in the section "What Is the Person Doing" in Chapter 11.

You can find a positive correlation between the annual number of fires in a city and the amount of money the city spends on its fire department. Does the regression line tell you how cities "really" deal with their fire departments? Some cities turn over their fire protection to private contractors. Some have volunteer departments. Are those cities showing erroneous deviations from an underlying relation?

INDIVIDUAL PURPOSES

People are not static entities. They are always active, always going somewhere. Suppose you could ask two trains, "Are you standing to the north or to the south?" A train stopped in Chicago would answer "north" and one stopped in Little Rock would answer "south." Then, if you were using the reasoning of correlation, you would conclude that the two trains were operating on a north-south track. But they might actually be going east and west, one to Detroit and the other to Las Vegas.

Neither the dot in the scatter-plot nor the correlation calculation can tell us that any individual is moving to keep the two variables connected in the manner of the regression line. One may be going to Detroit and the other to Las Vegas.

Here is a less fanciful example. Suppose you have the four questions below, and two people *both* give you the four answers shown at the right.

Is the work easy or hard?	Easy
Do you like the work to be easy or hard?	Hard
Do you get strict or permissive supervision?	Strict
Do you prefer strict supervision or permissive?	Permissive

The first person might give those answers because she is trying to maintain the pleasures of her own achievement. She wants to work at difficult tasks that test her mettle. She wants permissive supervision so that she can easily find challenging tasks and not find herself pressed into easy and therefore dull routines. The second person might give the same answers because he is trying to reach a level of financial income that is higher than his present salary. He wants harder work, even though he does not like hard work much, because he thinks that would give him a claim to higher pay. He wants permissive supervision so that he can select tasks that will show off his best talents. When people see those talents more clearly, he thinks, they will see more clearly why he should get more pay. Those are very different people, even though they gave identical answers and would show up at the very same place in a scatter-plot.

A correlation between two questions, a regression line, or a dimension through a cluster of questions is built mathematically by arbitrarily taking the direction through the longest stretch of the cloud of points to represent or typify the entire cloud in a simplified way. To illustrate with the extreme case, suppose we had only two persons and correspondingly only two points. Then we would assume that one point pinned down one end of the dimension (or relation or regression line) and the other point pinned down the other end. That is like the analogy of the two trains I gave earlier.

Nobody, of course, ever calculates a correlation for two points. And every point in the cloud has something to say, so to speak, about where the regression line lies. There is nothing, however, in the answer of any person taken alone that points toward the answers of any of the other people. (Very rarely indeed do questionnaire writers ask a question such as "Do you want the same thing as Joe?") There is no evidence in correlational data whatever that any individual person's answers (or any other behavior those answers might stand for) are guided by a regression line—a line from which the data-points have the least mean squared deviation. There is no evidence that "more" along that dimension (the regression line) would be "more" to some internal standard of any one person. The dimension inside any particular individual—the dimension that can vary from less to more according to some *internal* standard—may go in quite a different direction from the one constructed by the correlation. In brief, there is no way of knowing from a correlation coefficient or a scatter-plot how many of the pairs of scores are there because of the presumed lawful interaction of the two measured variables. There is nothing in a correlation over people to point to any necessity in the behavior of any single person.

In sum, when you take a cloud of points as evidence that the people from whom you got the data were guiding their behavior according to the regression line, you are assuming (1) that the actual behavioral relation between the variables is one-to-one, not one-to-many like that between bus riders and seats, (2) that every single individual was guiding his or her behavior in the manner of the regression line, and (3) that deviations from the regression line would not occur if only measurements were exact and unmeasured variables were not affecting different individuals differently. The correlational data give you no evidence whatever for any of those matters. You can treat the regression line as evidence only if you are willing to make all those shaky assumptions. Those are not the only strange assumptions that underlie the attempt to discover what goes on in humans by inspecting the entrails of correlation coefficients, but they should suffice to show my argument.

Instead of correlating over people, you can also correlate over moments, taking all the data from a single person. Some of the remarks I have made here do not apply to correlations taken over moments. I will not take space for the subtleties here, but a few of the uses of correlations over moments will appear in Chapter 11.

COMPLEX ANALYSES

The technique of correlation has become immensely elaborated to partial, multiple, rank-order, and intraclass correlations, to multiple regressions, to discriminant analysis, to factor analysis, to multidimensional scaling, and to other extensions of the original idea. All these techniques add assumptions. I will give you only one example from the many ways social scientists can become embrangled in the wonders of statistical analyses. Winne (1983, pp. 1-2) says that when you use multiple regression analysis, you will almost always end studying variables that are *not* the variables you started with:

> Multiple regression analysis does not describe relations among variables that represent constructs originally chosen by the researcher (except in one unlikely case; namely, when predictors are mutally correlated). Rather, these techniques create entirely new variables that represent different constructs. Multiple regression represents relations among these *new* variables and their latent constructs. . . . When the researcher unwittingly ascribes the same meaning to these new variables that have been created by the analysis as was appropriately applied to the original variables, policy or theory may be misdirected.

In other words, researchers who toss their data into a computer and order up a multiple regression analysis are sending themselves on a wild goose chase. And if you think that is flabbergasting, wait until you see my quotation from Corder-Bolz in Chapter 7.

SUMMARY

To calculate a correlation over a collection of people and act as if it tells us something about what goes on inside people, we must assume that (or act as if) every person assigned a pair of scores was acting in reference to the two variables (or more) that we chose to measure, that deviations from some single-valued function are "error," and that the least-squares criterion will find for us the relation from which the scores are deviating. We must act as if people who do not in fact (in the data) conform to those assumptions are actually doing so—or are trying to do so but are thwarted by happenstance. Once again, the method of relative frequencies seduces us into substituting assumptions for data.

6

Using Words

Social scientists rely heavily on words. All scientists rely on words to report results and in the hope of influencing other scientists. But social scientists rely heavily on words when coaxing people to let themselves be observed or to answer questions; they rely on words when giving instructions to subjects; and they often rely on words to carry information from subject to researcher. Some studies can be done without words—for example, watching the movement of crowds from the top of a tall building or ascertaining the proportion of people who violate a sign reading "Do not enter." But most studies rely on words. Here I will describe some difficulties and complexities in using words to get information about people. I will hang my disguisition on an example.

EXAMPLE

Suppose we have a supervisor and five workers. The six of them might work in a factory, a school, an insurance company, an automobile repair shop, a city bus line, or some other kind of organization. Suppose the supervisor is finding that things are not going right. Things do not get done when he thinks they should. Sometimes workers do things not in their job descriptions. Workers make complaints that puzzle him. He cannot figure out what the workers really want.

The supervisor asks the workers what is troubling them. He can understand some of the things they tell him, other things he cannot. Some workers mention things that seem to him too small to matter to anybody. He has the feeling that some workers are hiding what is bothering them the most. Some put him off with remarks like, "Oh, things are OK. I was just in a bad mood yesterday."

When the supervisor tries to figure out what the workers are reacting against, his guesses are naturally limited by what he can conceive—by the ideas he has about the features of working that workers can like or dislike. He may, for example, believe that the only thing that affects the satisfaction of workers is whether the work is hard or easy. His ideas may be even simpler than that: he may believe that all workers like to be kept busy, or he may believe that all workers like to have it easy. Or he may believe that supervision can vary only in one way: it can be strict or permissive. He may believe that workers (without asking himself whether he means some or most or all) like to be told what to do or that they like to do things their own way.

Suppose none of the five workers is encountering any frustration that he or she cannot easily cope with in dealing with tools, shop-floor layout, materials, schedules, or the like. Suppose instead that all of them are chafing under the kind of supervision they are getting. And suppose, to simplify matters, that there are chiefly two features or dimensions of the supervisor's style they are all acting against: (1) the frequency with which the supervisor tells them how well they are performing and (2) the amount of work they carry out jointly with one another.

And suppose that the five workers prefer different amounts of those two variables or dimensions. Letting one dimension run one way on the paper and the other in the other direction, we can represent in Figure 6.1 the efforts of the workers to control what they perceive they are getting from the supervisor. Assuming that the supervisor treats all the workers alike and that they perceive it that way, I have put the tails of the arrows all on one spot. The direction of an arrow shows the direction in which the worker is striving. For each worker, the supervisor's behavior has at present the mixture of the two dimensions at the tail of the arrow, and the worker would like the behavior to have the mix at the head of the arrow. The actions that baffle and annoy the supervisor are those by which the worker is trying to get the treatment (actually the perception of it) represented by the head of the arrow. Since the arrows go in such diverse directions, it is no wonder the supervisor is confused as long as he keeps wondering what the workers as a group want—as long as he keeps hoping he can find one thing to do that will satisfy all of them.

But at this point the supervisor has no picture in his head like the diagram. He has no thoughts, or no more than fleeting ones, about the two dimensions I mentioned. All he has are complaints that do not add up to anything that makes sense to him, absences with flimsy excuses, and veiled answers to his questions. What can the supervisor do after his questioning of the workers has got him no further along? He could simply shout at the workers that he will not stand for any more silly complaints, missed deadlines, or weakly explained absences. I won't take space to comment on that tactic.

Figure 6.1
Counteractions in Two Dimensions by Five Employees

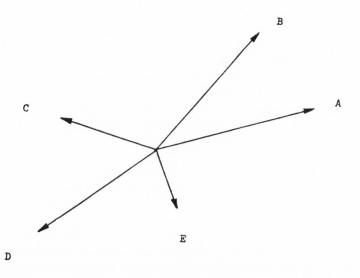

A common way to deal with this kind of difficulty is to try to get more information in words. Especially if you are dealing with enough people so that the information they give can remain anonymous, say a hundred or a thousand or at least a couple of dozen, you can get some outsiders to conduct interviews or hand out questionnaires. What kind of question might the outsiders ask? If you, an outsider, knew or guessed right that the two chief dimensions specifying the disturbances to the workers were the two I have specified here (for example) and if you could measure them accurately, then you would be in fine shape. But at second thought, no, you would not be. The workers would have to know the dimensions, too. They would have to be aware of what they were yearning for and know what was disturbing them. Then you would have to be skillful in using words that would bring those dimensions into the workers' minds. And then the workers would have to trust you to keep their answers confidential. If all those conditions could be brought about (and doing so is not easy), and if you did indeed know the dimensions—the "response space"—then you would be in good shape.

But you, the outsider, do not know the dimensions. You know only what the supervisor can tell you—which amounts to little more than "Something is wrong here." So what can you do?

QUESTIONING ABOUT SATISFACTION

One thing you can do, a common tactic, is to ask the workers, "How satisfied would you say you are with your present job?" And you could offer answers like "very," "somewhat," and so on. If every respondent means about the same thing by the words *very* and *somewhat*, you would then have some relative data (one respondent's satisfaction relative to another's) on the strengths of satisfaction or dissatisfaction. But three important things would remain unknown.

First, you would not know what the workers were satisfied or dissatisfied about. Of the potential information represented in Figure 6.1, you would have got only the relative lengths of the vectors. You would not have got their directions, and you would not know to whom they belonged (since you assured the respondents anonymity). In effect, you would have collapsed the two-dimensional space into one dimension, that of satisfaction or dissatisfaction regardless of source. You would know only that some people are more satisfied (or dissatisfied) than others. You already knew that.

Second, you would not know the behavioral strength, so to speak, of the answers. Of the behavior the supervisor described to you, which actions correspond to "very dissatisfied"? And are there actions of which the supervisor is unaware that correspond to "very dissatisfied"? Are some workers, for example, hunting actively for other jobs? Is someone building a bomb to go off next week? You do not have much of a guess about how hard the workers are striving to move in their desired directions. Some workers may be coping rather easily with the disturbances they get from the supervisor; the counteractions they take may distract them very little from their daily work and cause them only passing distress. Others may spend the bulk of their days and portions of their nights trying to figure out ways to counteract the supervisor's interference with what they want life at work to be like. You have no idea about that.

You would not know, either, what "very satisfied" means. To say it another way, the respondent's answer may not be anchored in the respondent's most preferred condition. For example, if I find my job boring but think it could never be otherwise, if I think that any job I could get would be equally boring, and if I am resigned to holding this kind of job for the rest of my life, then "very satisfied" could mean "about all I can expect." If, in contrast, my job is boring but I am taking a correspondence course in the hope of making it big in computers, then I am going to give a less favorable answer. Social scientists have some fancy names for that kind of comparison: relative deprivation, adaptation level, rising expectations, and the like.

Third, you would not know who is satisfied and who is dissatisfied, since you told the workers they need not put their names on the questionnaire. Even if you had asked them to do so, you could not ethically then go to them individually for more information or try to do something about their dissatisfaction, because most of them would take that as a breach of your promise of confidentiality. And if you had not promised confidentiality, you probably would have received more of the kind of veiled answers the supervisor had been getting.

What can you do with the information about satisfaction? If everyone answered "very satisfied," you can congratulate somebody. If everyone answered "very dissatisfied," you can worry. If the answers varied, as illustrated in Figure 6.1, you had better not jump to a conclusion, because you do not know anything about the directions in which they varied.

MULTIDIMENSIONAL QUESTIONING

Another thing you can do, also common, is to use factor analysis or multi-dimensional scaling. You would start by thinking up questions about all the kinds of conditions you think might affect the satisfaction of workers. For example:

How hard or easy is your work?

Do you like your work to be hard or easy?

Is your supervisor strict or permissive?

Do you like supervision to be strict or permissive?

How often does your supervisor let you know how well you are performing in your job?

How satisfied are you with the amount of information you get about how well you are performing?

To what extent do you have to depend on what others do to carry out your work?

After getting answers to your questions, you could calculate correlations over people among the answers to all the questions. You would find one or more (usually more) clusters of questions with fairly high intercorrelations. Within a cluster, that is, people who answered "yes" or "very much" to one question would answer "yes" or "very much" to most of the other questions, and people who answered "no" or "very little" to one would answer "no" or "very little" to most of the others. Going back to Figure 6.1, workers A and B might say "no" to a question that asked whether they were getting enough information from the supervisor about their performance. Person D would answer, "I am getting too much of that," to that question.

What can you learn from those clusters of correlated questions? There are certain things you can learn, but your confidence in what you learn will depend heavily on certain requirements or assumptions.

REQUIREMENTS

There are many pitfalls. I list below the requirements that I think must be met if the language between researcher and respondent is to serve the research-er's purposes. I may have overlooked a few. If the researcher does not deal explicitly with the requirements, but acts in the hope they are met, then of course they become assumptions.

1. The respondents must interpret the questions much as you meant them.

2. They must agree with you and with one another about the meaning of answers like "very" and "somewhat." Alternatively, when you do not give them specific answers to choose from but let them choose their own words, you must be able to discern what they mean.

3. They (and you) must be well informed about factual matters explicit or implicit in the questions.

4. Respondents must be sufficiently aware of their own purposes and possible ways they can see of pursuing them so that they can see clues to those purposes and paths in the questions and choose an answer like "yes" or "no" instead of choosing an answer like "doesn't matter," skipping the question as irrelevant, or marking some answer just to be marking one.

5. If you are hunting for relations or dimensions of behavior, a question must not be such as to draw the same answer from all the respondents. Each question must draw a range of response.

6. In some methods of data-collection and analysis, various technical requirements must be satisfied, of which I will mention only one as an example: the ratio of the number of questions to the number of respondents.

7. Respondents must trust you not to misuse the information they give you; they must not want to hide information from you.

What do I mean by agreeing on the meaning of words? That is a very elusive idea and one about which many books have been written. I think I mean that if two persons observe some event and both think a string of words adequately matches it, then they agree about the string of words. That specification contains lots of subtleties, but I will not go into them here. Pollsters and survey researchers are well aware of the great difficulties in transmitting meaning from researcher to respondent and back again.

What do I mean by factual matters explicit or implicit in the question? You might be studying preferences in taste and ask, "Which do you ordinarily like better, strawberry or pistachio ice cream?" There you would assume that the respondents were informed about those tastes you have explicitly mentioned—that they had experienced them.

In addition to the requirements I have listed, a very great difficulty social scientists encounter in relying on language is the loose correspondence between a stated intention and later action. The correspondence is loose even when the intention comes spontaneously from the subject (not in answer to a question or prod) and when the matter at hand is uncomplicated by threats or emotions. But that loose correspondence is a matter for specific theory. It is a realm of behavior you can try to study with any method you like. Because it is not a matter embedded in method, I did not put it in my list of requirements.

MULTIDIMENSIONAL QUESTIONING CONTINUED

My list of requirements may seem difficult to satisfy before you can put confidence in what your factor analysis or multidimensional scaling might tell you. It is indeed a long list of tough requirements, and not often are more than two or three of them met when researchers try to find out what is bothering people by using questionnaires or interviews. But for the moment, let us suppose you have met them all.

What Do You Learn?

What do you learn from your multidimensional analysis? First, instead of having a single question about satisfaction, you now have answers to a variety of questions. Even without going to the trouble of a factor analysis or multidimensional scaling, you can look among those questions for clusters in each person's answers. You might get a clue or two about purposes the person wants most to pursue. This is a very inefficient way to hunt for purposes and preferred inputs from the environment, but you might make a lucky guess.

Second, among 30 or 100 people, you might find a large number of them yielding clusters of items; that is, answering "yes" to almost all of the items in a cluster or answering "no" to almost all. By studying the questions in the cluster, you might be able to make better guesses about the kinds of perceptions of their worlds at least *some* of those people are trying to maintain. There are numerous subtleties that arise in the use of multidimensional analysis, but I won't take space for them in this book.

The third thing you might get from your analysis of the data is an estimate, a minimal estimate anyway, of the ways the people differ from one another in what they are attracted by or want to stay away from. You get a minimal estimate, in other words, of the number of dimensions of the "response space," as it is called. Finding many dimensions would prevent you from thinking that things are simpler than they are. On the other hand, you might be lucky enough to get a "space" in which most of the answers could fit along a single dimension. That could make it easier for you to get still further information. You might find it profitable in some circumstances to learn one or more of those three kinds of things. You can be confident of what you have learned, however, only to the extent that you have met the requirements I listed earlier.

In sum, if you wanted to help the supervisor make headway in solving his problem, then to the extent that the seven conditions I listed earlier are satisfied, you might get some good clues from a multidimensional analysis to give you a good start in using the method of specimens. But that's about all.

Using interviews and questionnaires is not always a waste of time. Used judiciously, they can save you a lot of time and backtracking, and they can give you some directions along which to start other kinds of action. In successful applications, consultants take the analysis of the answers to groups of managers and workers and ask them what ideas the results bring up in their own minds about themselves and their work. Sometimes the consultants get confirmation of some of their analysis and further elaborations of meaning. Sometimes consultants get information that reveals faults or weaknesses in their analysis, almost always stemming from a failure of one of the seven requirements to hold.

Using the directions of dissatisfaction that are confirmed and any others that may come out of thorough discussion, consultants can then help groups to work out solutions to problems—that is, events in the shared environment that are causing people to expend too much energy in pursuing their purposes. In successful problem-solving, individuals reveal enough information about the kinds of events they act *against* that the discussions, simulations, and exercises become an approximation of the method of specimens.

What Do You Not Learn?

What do you *not* learn from your multidimensional analysis? First, to the extent that one or more of the seven requirements does not hold, what you learn gets closer and closer to zero. If I were allotting space here according to the amount of trouble researchers can make for themselves by making unwarranted assumptions, I would fill up a whole chapter simply repeating that last sentence over and over. But I hope I can convey the same emphasis by asking you to go back to the section on "Requirements" and ask yourself how many studies in social science you know about in which the researcher demonstrated that those requirements, or even most of them, were met.

Second, although you get some clues to what might be causing satisfaction or dissatisfaction somewhere among the people in the group, you get only very weak clues to locating the individuals who might be feeling the largest gaps between how things are now and how they would like them to be. What you get from the respondents is *language*. They tell you *about* their own perceptions of their behavior or their predictions of it. You can be sure that many respondents are wrong in estimating their own purposes and gaps, but you have not learned even who is making the best or worst estimates, not to speak of what more correct estimates would be like.

Having asked a variety of questions does not help you to know the kind or strength of the behavior that might correspond to the answers. The answers to the individual items do not tell you; you do not know whether "a lot" corresponds to fuming inwardly, arguing hard with the boss, or sabotaging the assembly line. Neither do the strengths of the correlations tell you. For example, a strong correlation between two variables does not tell you that people who are fighting hard to maintain one kind of environmental condition are fighting hard to maintain the other. The strength of a correlation depends on whether, when you order the people by their scores on one variable, you get the same ordering of scores on the other variable. The absolute levels of the scores have nothing to do with it.

You will be misled, too, because the multidimensional analysis (any, at least, with which I am acquainted) substitutes people for one another in the manner I described in Chapter 5.

Third, you do not know how much the picture you get from your analysis is shaped by your theory of what is relevant to the workers. You might have guessed wrong about the questions to include. You might have left out some questions about events or conditions that a lot of workers are trying hard to counteract.

Fourth, although you can calculate a resultant or mean, that would be a very poor guide to action, even a dangerous one. You might be tempted to act upon it. You might think, "Well, I know that if we move the conditions to the resultant (the vector average) of where everyone wants to go, we will not be pleasing everyone, but at least things will be somewhat closer to what they want." That conclusion is wrong. Look back at Figure 6.1. If conditions were free to move to the point of balance among the tugs being applied by the five people, they would settle down at a point between A and B at the end of a vector about half as long as those two. If you were to move the conditions to that point, you would please persons A and B to some extent, but you would go in the wrong direction for the majority of the persons: C, D, and E. Persons A and B would complain somewhat less, but the rest would complain more.

CODA

Language is marvelously handy. It can save a great deal of traipsing about watching people. But it is also chancy. It is chock full of slippages between what you think words stand for and the correspondence you hope for in your latest research or action. When we ask for verbal information, especially when we do it by writing multiple-choice questionnaire items, we usually hope that the image the respondents have of their situation and their possibilities for action is the same as the image we have. The hope is usually futile.

The best you can do with interviews and questionnaires designed to bring quick answers from a large number of people is to get some clues about perceptions of their environments that *some* of them might be trying to maintain. But you will not know which of them are trying to maintain which, even if they put their names on the questionnaire.

When giving instructions to subjects, researchers often seem to assume that subjects respond solely to the content the experimenters hope they have put into words, not to the situation itself. They often seem to assume that no subject will need to take note, for example, of a situation in which it is apparently legitimate for experimenters to talk to them about certain topics in a demanding way (please read this, please answer this), or of a cultural custom of doing what you are told by a person standing in front of the room, or (as may be the case) of the fact of the other subjects' being close to their own age or in similar occupations. Most teachers know that teenagers are adept at doing superficially what the teacher wants despite not having heard more than three words of what the teacher has said. Most youngsters retain that skill for the rest of their lives. Most researchers seem to think their subjects have forgotten it. The situation puts meaning on the experimenter's words. The context is written, so to speak, into the experimenter's instructions to the subjects.

In most research in social science, some use of language is unavoidable, and sometimes it must be relied upon rather heavily if any investigation at all is to be done. Sometimes, however, I think we use language simply because we are too impatient or are unwilling to spend enough time or money on a more direct method. Perhaps because of an eagerness to collect data quickly, professional researchers often, for example, ask subjects what they think they would do in certain situations in the hope of discovering what they would indeed do. But, everyday researchers (our co-workers, for example) are not above watching for days and months the behavior of the people they want to learn about. Some of them, such as personnel directors, often keep meticulous records of their observations.

If you are studying language, then of course language must be a large part of your study. But even there, you can reduce the uncertainties if you avoid using language to learn about the uses of language. Linguists and cultural anthropologists know some ways of doing that. A minuscule example is the one in the first paragraph of this chapter: counting the people who violate a sign reading "Do not enter."

To the extent that researchers can reduce their use of language to a minimum in setting up experiments and taking data, they can reduce making the assumptions that are necessary when the requirements I listed earlier are not satisfied— and those requirements are indeed very hard to satisfy. In Chapter 11, I will describe several experiments in which reliance on language was minimal.

SUMMARY

In trying to find out how people function in a situation, to find out what is happening in a way that suits them and what they want to alter, a simple thing one can do is to ask them, in effect, "How's it going?" People who study life in human organizations (including workaday researchers) do essentially that when they ask workers about satisfaction. Even if you can meet all the requirements of using language, doing that does not tell you much.

To explore the possibilities in more detail, you can think up a lot of questions referring to various possible relationships between the worker and the working situation. You can then score the questions in some way and run correlations among them over the people. If you find that all the correlations are low and there is no clustering among the questions, you learn nothing except the lists of answers to the lists of questions. For practical purposes, of course, one can sometimes find some nuggets of useful information in the lists.

If some items do cluster, you can get some clues to what might be bothering some of the people, though you will not know which satisfactions or frustrations are connected to which people. You can also get an estimate of how varied are the kinds of conditions the people want to maintain or bring about. That is sometimes useful in estimating the necessary complexity of the solution to a problem. The confidence you can put in what you have learned depends on whether you have met the requirements for using language I listed in the section headed "Requirements."

To the extent that researchers can reduce their use of language to a minumum in setting up experiments and in taking data, they can reduce making the assumptions that are necessary when the requirements I listed are not satisfied.

7

Fine Slicing

The underlying conception of causation in the method of relative frequencies has often been symbolized as *S-O-R*, for stimulus-organism-response, where the stimulus *(S)* is a cause and the response *(R)* is an effect. The conception is one of input causing output, as when you frighten *(S)* a cat *(O)* and the cat defecates *(R)* or as when you put a coin *(S)* into a vending machine *(O)* and it puts out a cup of coffee *(R)*. I will discuss that conception of linear causation at greater length in the next chapter. Here, my point is that studying human action as if it can be understood in separate episodes or slices encourages researchers to believe they can understand more and more by slicing the episodes thinner and thinner.

With the theory (or metatheory) of *S-O-R*, researchers would be delighted to find that at one level of input variable *X*, all the observed people produce output behavior *Y*, and at another level of *X*, they do not. That delightfully simple hope is represented by the simplest contingency table:

```
                              Y
                       No          Yes
                      -----       -----
            High       a           b
     X
            Low        c           d
```

If that hope were borne out, all the data would fall into cells *b* and *c*. With more values of *X* and *Y* (more rows and columns), all the data would fall into the cells lying along the diagonal. With continuous variables, all the data would fall on a line; that is, the correlation would be 1.0. But that kind of fall of data almost never happens. When it does miraculously happen, it fails to happen when the study is replicated.

THE EVENTUAL COMPENDIUM

When researchers find that their outcomes are muddied by the appearance of unwanted data in cells *a* and *d,* the metatheory underlying *S-O-R* makes the next step obvious. If behavior is controlled by input variables, then we can improve predictability by putting more "controls" on the behavior. We can find what else is controlling the behavior in addition to *X*. With the help of some further theory, we can choose another input variable X_2 and slice our collection of subjects into two parts according to whether they are high or low on X_2. Then, if life is simple and our new hope is borne out, we get the following distribution:

		Low slice on X_2				High slice on X_2	
		\<center\>Y\</center\>				\<center\>Y\</center\>	
		No	Yes			No	Yes
		-----	-----			-----	-----
X_1	High	a			High		b
	Low		d		Low	c	

All the behavior that had put data in cells *a* and *d* is now seen to occur only at the low value of X_2, and the behavior we originally predicted occurs only at the high value of X_2. We can now predict what every person will do if we have measured the person on X_1 and X_2. Science is wonderful.

But that never happens, either. We make still another slice, and another, and another. With correlations, we add more input variables to our partial and multiple correlations. We add more variables to our discriminant analyses and more items to our factor analyses.

Statisticians have gone about as far as they can go in providing us with clever ways of cutting up a domain of behavior in the hope that enough of the right input variables will predict the whole of the data taken on the output variable. Most of the techniques have been in use for decades. But we have yet to hear someone cry, "Eureka!"

Nevertheless, the reasoning of slicing finer and finer seems to lie behind what many, maybe most, social scientists mean when they talk about the cumulative progress of science. They seem to envision the eventual compendium as reading something like this: "Table XVIII shows how to predict *Y* from *X*.

People will act with a lot of Y if they are high on all of X_1, X_2, X_3, and so on through X_{23}. They will act with an intermediate amount of Y if they are low on X_1 through X_4 and X_{10} but high on the rest. And they will act with a low amount of Y if they are low on any seven or more of X_1 through X_{10} and on X_{17} through X_{23}. Just be careful to pick the right people or give them the right inputs, or both, so that the input variables, the X's, will be at the right levels.''

The idea seems to be that as the years and decades (and centuries?) go by, we will eventually discover the right slices to take in every domain of human behavior and will then be able to slice all the possibilities so finely that we will be able to predict the behavior of every person in every cell of the multidimensional contingency table.

Example

I will give a fictitious example now of what seems to me an ordinary range of diversity in the actions (outputs) people might choose by which to maintain similar inputs coming to them from a work environment. I think the diversity I have written into this example is quite ordinary, but it is nevertheless much greater than we typically find among the variables in single studies, even most programs of studies, in the social sciences.

Suppose we observe four machinists. Of the four, Angie is the quiet one. She seems taciturn, sometimes even dour. The foreman says to her, ''The day you say something more than 'Yes, sir,' I'll give everybody an hour off to celebrate.''

Paul is the most methodical and the neatest. He wipes off his bench and sweeps the floor around it several times a day. He spoils the fewest pieces of work. Today he spoiled one. The foreman says to him, ''Well, what do you know! Old Perfect Paul slipped up today!''

Darrell is the most loquacious. His volubility seems to soar when the foreman comes to talk to him. The foreman can hardly get a word in edgewise. The foreman says to him, ''What are you trying to do? Drown out the machinery?''

Catherine does good work, but she is often absent. She calls in sick often enough to keep her remaining sick leave close to zero, though she always seem to be in good health when she is at work. She uses up compensatory time as soon as possible. She was absent yesterday. Today the foreman says to her, ''Well, I see you're honoring the company with your gracious presence today.''

After observing a few more hours, we find that the remarks of the foreman are typical. He has a very sharp tongue. Only Darrell ever initiates conversation with him. Sometimes the machinists make derogatory remarks about him to one another.

Just as people extract from the ''same'' environmental event different aspects to be converted into perceptual input, so also they choose different actions through which to maintain the ''same'' perceptual input. In my fictitious example, I am supposing that all four machinists find the behavior of the foreman disturbing, and all want to reduce their experience of his biting remarks to zero. They all take actions containing some feature which, in interaction with some feature of the foreman's behavior, will enable them, they hope, to perceive a reduction in the foreman's biting remarks. The four choose different kinds of actions.

Angie tries to attract the foreman's attention as little as possible. If he talks to her, she uses replies that she hopes will end the conversation quickly. She reduces her own talking to a minimum in the hope of discouraging the foreman from talking. Paul tries to give the foreman no occasion for talk. He tries to do his work so well that the foreman will have no reason to talk to him. Darrell tries to give the foreman no opening in his own flow of words. When the foreman comes around, he prattles on, hoping the foreman will give up trying to get a word in and go away. Catherine simply stays away from the foreman by staying away from work as much as possible. The four are all trying to alter the "same" input, but they use the environmental resources in different ways.

If you were trying to connect inputs with outputs, those four machinists would certainly discourage you. Even if you had been lucky enough to hit upon the abrasive features of the foreman's behavior as your independent variable, the ensuing actions would seem to scatter in very different directions. One person chooses taciturnity, another talkativeness, another proficiency, and another absence. The same stimulus seems to produce very different responses. No lawfulness is apparent.

You might say, well, we can control for all the moderating and intervening variables. You can rather easily think of circumstances and personal qualities that could make it easier for one machinist to choose one kind of action and another another. You might speculate that Angie chose reticence because, unlike Paul, she did not have exceptional skill as a machinist and because, unlike Darrell, she was not facile in speaking (maybe English was her second language) and because she was not as healthy as Catherine and needed to save up her sick leave for actual illnesses. You might speculate, too, that she had a desperate need for her job and could not risk telling the foreman she would begin a grievance procedure unless he mended his ways; that for the same reason, she did not complain to the foreman's boss; that she could not very often hear what the foreman was saying to the others, thought the foreman was picking mostly on her, was ashamed of it, and did not want to attract the attention of the others by more noisy or visible actions; that she did not try to persuade the foreman to be more polite, because she thought that would only give him more opportunity to make nasty remarks; that she did not try to hit the foreman with a baseball bat, because there was no baseball bat on the premises; that she did not hit him with a wrench, because she thought she might lose the fight; that she did not ask to be transferred to another foreman, because those four machinists, with their foreman, comprised the only machining department in the plant; that she did not offer the foreman sexual favors or put arsenic in his lunch, because she had internal standards restraining her from those actions; and so on.

You can probably think of twenty more kinds of action Angie might have taken, along with corresponding conditions that could have discouraged her from taking them, to reduce her suffering the foreman's biting remarks. You can probably think of twenty more kinds of action that Paul, Darrell, and Catherine might have taken. To "control" for all those moderating and intervening conditions, you would have to know a lot about Angie, about the people around her, about the organization of the plant and its norms, about the physical layout, and so on.

I have illustrated some of the possibilities only at the point of output action. At the point of input, we would have to cope with a similarly large number of possible features of the foreman's behavior that Angie and the others might perceive in addition to his abrasiveness.

Turning to the internal standards higher up in the neural hierarchy that might control the input from the foreman's actions differently in Angie, Paul, Darrell, and Catherine, we would again find multitudinous possibilities. Internal standards for being helpful to others, for taking interpersonal risks, for enduring harassment, for maintaining employment opportunities, for maintaining calm, for suffering persecution on earth as the path to peace in heaven, for proper respect for superiors—those standards and many others could affect the kind of input perceived, the degree of discrepancy between the amount of the foreman's abrasiveness to be tolerated and the perception of its actual amount, and the choice of environmental path through which to reduce the abrasiveness.

Multiplying the possible relevant aspects that four or four hundred humans might perceive in an environmental event by the events an environment might produce, then by the possible internal standards that might be compared with the perception, then by the possible degrees of discrepancy between perception and standard, then by the available resources in the environment through which to select suitable action, and then by the efficacy of the action, we get a number of cross-combinations of conditions so large as to be absurd to contemplate. But though that number brings absurdity to the experimentalist trying to work only with inputs and outputs, it also brings us awe and humility in contemplating the potentialities of humankind.

I hope that example of the machinists makes clear the gargantuan sizes of contingency tables, or the gargantuan numbers of control groups, or the gargantuan lists of variables in multiple regressions that the advocates of fine slicing seem willing to contemplate. Furthermore, my example was a static one; it said nothing about how *changes* in some X's might affect other X's—about dynamic interactions among variables. Studying dynamic interactions requires at least transition matrices and, better yet, the differential calculus.

I suppose some researchers are still doggedly hunting for the few golden variables that will account for all the behavior. But that is not what I see published. What I see is fine slicing.

TROUBLES WITH FINE SLICING

It seems obvious to me that the grand plan embraced by those who practice fine slicing faces formidable difficulties. Here is a quick review of some of them.

Multitudes of Variables

In the realms of human behavior in which the method of relative frequencies has been used during the past several decades to hunt for reliable predictions, I know of none that shows any sign of having come upon a few variables that will account for all or even almost all the variance even among the variables interesting to social scientists, to say nothing of further variables that would be valuable to know about in a practical situation. On the contrary, the journals continue to be full of reports of trials of another and another cluster of input variables, most of which show the same poor success at prediction to which we have become accustomed. I see no evidence that slicing with more and more variables promises to improve our ability to predict behavior well. I see nothing in the record of the past hundred years to encourage us to set out to make comparisons among hundreds and thousands of groups of multiply measured subjects.

Using Words

In Chapter 6, I gave a list of seven requirements on the use of language that researchers must satisfy if they are to avoid assumptions about what is happening in a study—assumptions guaranteed to be wrong at least to some extent and often very wrong. Variations in the meaning conveyed by language from the researcher to this and that subject, variations among regions of a country, among occupational groups, and from decade to decade and sometimes even year to year all affect outcomes. When language is used to measure variables or to specify the dimensions of behavior requested of subjects, those variations actually change the variables by which the domain of behavior is being sliced—reducing, often severely, the comparability of one study with another. Most of the seven requirements are usually very difficult to satisfy. But leaving even one of them to assumption can leave unknown a large part of what actually happened in a study.

In addition to those difficulties, more are added by the unavoidable use of language in reporting. If one researcher wants to study the same topic as another, the later researcher must usually get the information about the earlier study from a written report. Once in a while (not often enough), researchers supplement what they read in a report by writing a letter or calling on the telephone. Sometimes, perhaps as a student or as a member of a team of researchers, they have been actually present at an earlier study. The great bulk of the transmission of information about studies, however, goes through written language. There are always gaps, usually great gaps, between the information appearing in a research report and what the next researcher will need to know.

Internal Standards

If one thing is certain, it is that however convenient it may be to conceive an internal standard and give it the same name for every human in some collection, we will actually find as many standards as there are individuals. Though many will be very similar as far as we can ascertain, every one will be unique in some way. That means that not every subject will find an experimental condition (treatment, manipulation) relevant to the internal standards the researcher hopes to affect; not every subject will feel called upon to "respond."

The method of relative frequencies has no way of ascertaining the uniqueness of an internal standard in an individual and no way of ascertaining the hierarchy of standards in an individual, and therefore no way of making the slices that would be necessary to segregate individuals with those differing individual characteristics that would affect how they would deal with an environmental input. Those differences, like others, do no harm to the logic or practice of casting a net, but they put ineradicable uncertainty into fine slicing.

Calibration

Some psychological measurements are taken in units of grams, centimeters, and seconds. That occurs mostly in psychophysics and physiological psychology. It is done in studies of color vision, of auditory perception, of uses of muscles in movement, of operating knobs and buttons on machinery, and so on. But in great reaches of personality, social psychology, educational psychology, and clinical psychology, not to speak of sociology and politics, the only unit available is the standard deviation. That is not good enough for accurate fine slicing, because the physical units (or even the count of number of items "right") corresponding to a standard deviation change with every new sample of subjects. It is not good enough for practical applications, either. The person of practical affairs, perhaps an officer of a company contemplating a project to change managerial style, will not be grateful to hear, "When the anxiety level of 30 percent of the participants in your change project exceeds 1.3 standard deviations (calculated from a population of people like yours), provide them with at least 1.7 standard deviations of social support."

The slicing will go wrong, too, because the method of relative frequencies is bound to put some people into the wrong slice. I showed in Chapter 4 how the submethod of control groups is incapable of locating any single person in a particular cell of the contingency table or scatter-plot. I pointed out in Chapter 5 how the relation between two variables (correlation) must almost always be derived partly from people whose behavior is *not* guided by one or the other of the two variables, maybe not by either one.

STATISTICAL RELIABILITY OF CHANGE

Within the method of relative frequencies, the difficulty of reaching a confident conclusion that a "real" change has occurred has plagued methodologists for years. When you rely on the mathematics of probability to demonstrate change, you want to show that the sample after change would be drawn randomly from the population to which the pre-change sample belongs only with a very small probability. But when applied to change in samples, the mathematics of probability and the possible sources of "error" and bias get horribly complicated. The literature contains many examinations of the probabilistic implications of statistics on change scores; almost all end with admonitions not to base conclusions on one or another simple, straightforward, easily understood statistical analysis. A high point in that literature, I think, was the 1978 paper by Corder-Bolz reporting a series of Monte Carlo studies of six statistical procedures designed to draw defensible conclusions from change scores. He concluded:

> Analysis of covariance and analysis of variance of residualized gain scores appear to be entirely inappropriate. Multiple factor analysis of variance models utilizing pretest and posttest scores appear to yield invalid F ratios. The analysis of variance of different scores and the multiple factor analysis of variance using repeated measures are the only models which can adequately control for pre-treatment differences; however, they appear to be robust only when the error level is 50 percent or more. This places serious doubt regarding published findings and theories based upon change score analysis. (p. 22)

Think of that. Corder-Bolz is saying, I think, that if you want to go beyond cataloging static states to discover the ways behavior changes, and if you want an estimate of change not biased toward too much or too little, then you must give up any hope of precision and flood your data with at least 50 percent error! How can you succeed at fine slicing if you must make a choice between biased slicing and data pervaded by error?

Dynamics

The method of relative frequencies contains no effective way of charting the flow of events, of tracking change from moment to moment. The times of observation must be separated by at least the amount of time it takes to take measurements, and the measurements are often lengthy. If behavior must be observed while it flows, the measurements are usually too intrusive to be used.

In addition to moment-to-moment twists and turns, there is also the difficulty of changes over longer periods of time: the matter of generalizing to changing populations. I wrote about this in Chapter 3. Social psychologists, sociologists, political scientists, economists, and the like are plagued with this difficulty, though I suppose historians welcome it. It is what Gergen (1973) wrote about.

The relations among our variables change faster than we might think. Many females perceive potentialities for themselves that few perceived 20 or 30 years ago. Although the majority of people in the United States probably still believe that competition is always an unmitigated good, the proportion is probably dropping. Some investigators say that the economic expectations of the very poor are probably becoming even more hopelessly pessimistic. The proportions among types of crime, including those committed in schools, have changed during the last three decades or so, and so on. Knowledge is always knowledge of the past; it can give us hypotheses to test in the present and future, but it cannot ever enable a consultant to prescribe out of an encyclopedia.

Nonrandom Sampling

None of the troubles I have mentioned above weakens to any serious degree the casting of nets, the compiling of catalogs, the writing of history, or getting clues to internal standards that might be operating in individuals. The net does not, of course, find *high* correlations for you. It finds merely whatever strengths of correlations that are there to find.

If, however, you are trying to *maximize* predictability by the strategy of fine slicing—if you are trying to find the categories within which you can predict every act—then the troubles I am listing do seriously jeopardize success. And nonrandom sampling messes up everything, including casting nets.

Most studies in social science do not use random samples of listed populations. The result is that a statistic from one sample does not predict very well the statistic from another sample, and there is no way to estimate the likelihood of the disparities. There is no way of estimating where the slice has been taken.

Diagnosis

In practical affairs, it is often sufficient for your purposes, as in the case of casting the net, to know that a certain percentage of your customers, with a specifiable range of uncertainty, will buy razor blades during the last quarter of the year or that a certain percentage of your students will drop out during the spring.

If you plan, however, to change the way you are organized to package and slip razor blades or to change the curriculum and the way you counsel students, you then want to predict with pretty high confidence the varieties of behavior you are likely to get, when they hear your ideas about change, from the people who run the packaging machines, the shipping clerks, the managers of your retail outlets, the teachers, the counselors, and the students. Being able to estimate the frequency of the most likely kind of behavior is not enough, and knowing the range of uncertainty of a mean does not help. It is nice to know that your bets are well placed, but you will not feel at ease until you have confidence that no person, not a single one, is going to do something that will ruin your entire project. That means that you will care little about what is likely to send most people into a tizzy, but will care a lot about what will send your own particular people into a tizzy. You must be able to get the right information about your particular people. Doing that is diagnosis.

You must have a pretty good idea about what will be the right information to look for, and you must be able to get the information soon enough for it to be useful and in a way that will not send the people into the very tizzy you want to avoid. If you can do that, your diagnosis will be timely and useful.

Some social psychologists tell us, for example, that personality characteristics will affect the dynamics of discussion or decision making in a group. They tell us that certain combinations of personality types will make certain outcomes more and less likely. To make use of that information, we must administer personality tests to the participants. Good heavens! First, by the time we get the personality tests administered and scored, the meeting is well on its way. Do we then say, "Hey, guys, let's start over"? Second, suppose we discover that the personality mix augurs a poor result. Do we call off the meeting? Third, if we want the right personality mix, whom do we test? How do we know whom to test before we have tested them? Do we test everybody in the company and then send the right mix of personalities to the meeting regardless of their positions? Do we test everyone at the time of entering the company and then assume that they will remain unchanged? Fourth, what about people whom we cannot coerce into taking the test? Suppose we need a meeting with some representatives of some other companies. Do we say to our visitors, "Before we start the meeting, ah, I wonder if you would, ah, fill out this, ah, personality test"?

Finally, measuring one psychological variable often changes another. Being tested is an environmental event with which persons must cope. If Alfred has his mind on going into a meeting to join others in solving a problem, and you ask him to answer a personality test, Alfred's picture of what is going on in his environment changes. In your fine slicing, you may have supposed Alfred to be at a certain level of, say, readiness to join others in solving a problem. But your measurement of his personality has now moved him out of that level of readiness into another. And you may also have altered several other variables having to do with his attitude toward the company, his self-esteem, and so on. You can see numerous ways in which fine slicing becomes very slippery in practical situations.

All the troubles I have listed above afflict fine slicing. Any one of them, I think, certainly any two, make the strategy of fine slicing a forlorn hope.

SUMMARY

Many social scientists believe that the findings of social science will accumulate, dovetail, illuminate one another, and eventually coalesce into a grand design that predicts everything worth predicting. If they intend to pursue the grand design with the method of relative frequencies, I think that vision is a chimera. For another argument that reaches the same conclusion (to select only one piece of writing among many), see MacIntyre (1984, Chapters 6, 7, 8).

If your purpose is to cast a net, compile a catalog, write history, or get clues to possible internal standards, the method of relative frequencies will serve you well. If, however, you hope to accumulate data (with a lot of help from your friends) to support an eventual list of highly predictive laws about the behavior of the human creature, then the assumptions you must make in adopting the method of relative frequencies for that enterprise will guarantee its failure.

I laid out a series of dubious assumptions in Chapters 4 through 7. Here are a few of them: that people can be substituted for one another—that is, that people in one situation (in a control group, for example) will act in the same way people in another situation do if they move to that situation (Chapter 4); that people who act contrary to our hypotheses are simply instances of "error" and would have acted according to hypothesis had we only been more clever in our experimental design and measurements (Chapter 4); that people over whom we choose to calculate a correlation are somehow "tending" to behave in the way represented by a line drawn through the longest dimension of the cloud of points; that they would have behaved that way except for "error" (Chapter 5); that all the people in a study will interpret the words you use the way you intend them when you give instructions and ask questions (Chapter 6); and that everything will hold still long enough so that you can learn by fine slicing more and more about smaller and smaller domains of behavior (Chapter 7).

You may have remained unconvinced by some of the arguments I have given. But if you are convinced that the method of relative frequencies requires us to act as if even a couple of those assumptions are true, and if you think those assumptions are as foolish as I do, then it seems to me that you must agree that the method is a hopeless way to search for the rules by which members of the human species function.

I have now almost finished with my exhibition of the assumptions underlying the method of relative frequencies. In Chapter 8, I will criticize the assumptions underlying the conception of linear causation. In Chapters 9 through 12, I will describe the use of the method of specimens in discovering the manner of functioning of the human creature.

III

Causation

Along with its conception of independent and dependent variables, a metatheory of straight-line, episodic causation underlies the method of relative frequencies. That view of causation has served well in the physical sciences, though some physicists do worry about it.

Living creatures behave very differently from lifeless things. Unlike a rock, a human does not just sit until something bumps it. Writing that, it startles me that I feel it necessary to make a point of such an already pointed fact.

The method of specimens makes it much easier to examine the behavior of living creatures, where causes arise simultaneously from the environment and from within the creature. The internal processes by which living beings deal with those causes are ceaseless, seamless, and circular.

Chapter 8 will review linear, straight-line causation. Chapter 9 will prepare the way for the method of specimens by describing the interactions of internal and external causes.

8

Linear Causation

The most pervasive and fateful assumption underlying the great bulk of the writings in social science (and underlying most lay thinking, too) is the assumption of linear, straight-line causality. Not only is that assumption not the only available one, but it is the wrong one with which to learn how living creatures manage to keep living.

The underlying conception of causation in the method of relative frequencies has often been symbolized as S-O-R, for stimulus-organism-response, where the stimulus (S) is a cause and the response(R) is an effect. The conception is one of input causing output, as when you kick (S) a can (O) and the can sails (R) to a new position—and stays there—or as when you prick (S) a person (O) and the person cries (R) "Ouch!"

In the most naive interpretation of the S-O-R, the conception is that the organism sits passively until some environmental event causes it to move. Then it does something, after which it sits waiting for another environmental event. On the face of it, that view of things seems too simple for anyone to believe. Nevertheless, you can find reports of studies in almost every issue of the professional journals of almost every social science that assume that simple scheme and no more. Furthermore, a great many practical people also hold to that simple theory. There are teachers who believe that students learn nothing until instructed to do so by teachers. There are managers who believe that workers will not work until prodded to do so by rewards and threats of punishment.

Most of the law assumes that some people must control the behavior (*R*) of other people (*O*) and that the control can be achieved by threats (*S*).

In a more sophisticated interpretation, theorists endow the person with the capacity to be selective about the environmental events to which the person will respond. The theory grants that humans have sense organs and memories; it postulates that the senses and the memories together screen out many perceived patterns, preventing any effect from them, while allowing others to produce action. Even this more complex kind of theory, however, if it clings to linear causation, must leave the initiative to the environment.

The assumption of linear causation has served physics very well. Non-living things, however, do not (with trivial exceptions) act to maintain their own integrity. When we move from non-living things, which behave according to entropy, to living things, which behave contrary to it, we should not be surprised to find linear causation inadequate to explain what we see.

ASSUMPTIONS

The *S-O-R* scheme requires three assumptions about the nature of things:

1. Cause comes before effect. As a corollary, cause and effect are separate, non-overlapping events.

2. Cause and effect appear in local, distinguishable episodes having a beginning and an ending. That is, your understanding of what has happened from cause to effect requires knowledge only of the events that occur from the beginning of the cause to the end of the effect. As a corollary, the beginning and the end are recognizable.

3. The laws of nature are everywhere the same. If an effect follows a cause anywhere, it will follow everywhere. More generally, if a law holds at one place or time, it will hold in every place and time.

If you are casting a net, compiling a catalog or a history, or even estimating a correlation in the next sample, then the first two assumptions are not necessary; they are irrevelant. You are using only the third assumption. That is no burden; that assumption underlies every science. But if you use the method of relative frequencies to conduct a causal experiment, then you are adopting all three.

VARIABLES

Instead of conceiving inputs and outputs as whole events, we can conceive them as changes in variables. The air temperature (*S*) in a room *rises*, and the person (*O*) *reduces* the number of layers (*R*) of clothing. The mother's upturned hand comes *closer* (*S*) to the baby (*O*), and the baby's hand with the rattle in

Figure 8.1
A Path Diagram

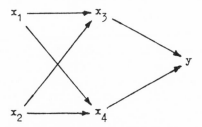

it moves *closer* (R) to the mother. The hostility (S) in the boss's voice and words *increases*, and the words per minute (R) of the subordinate (O) *decrease*.

The *S-O-R* scheme allows any number of starting and ending variables. It allows, that is, multiple causes and multiple effects. It allows any number of independent and moderator variables to originate in the external environment and any number of intervening variables to lie within the person. There may also be multiple actions as outcomes, from some of which researchers extract the dependent variables that interest them.

Thinking of variables instead of events enables us to put numbers on observations (to quantify them) and thereby make them more easily comparable from one experiment to another. With variables in mind, we can convert the *S-O-R* to *X-O-Y*. When researchers want to observe only various values of *X* and *Y*, they often find it convenient to drop the organism from the picture and think just about the relation between the variables: $X \rightarrow Y$. When we focus on variables, it is easy to forget that behavior does not exist separately from organisms—that humans are real, tangible creatures with real, tangible parts.

When we want to think about several variables at the same time, we can diagram the relations among them as in Figure 8.1, a sort of diagram nowadays called a "path diagram." Note that the living creature has vanished. We are no longer studying whole humans, but instead relations among variables. Often, indeed, researchers seem indifferent to the kind of organism or creature or assembly of creatures from whose behavior a variable has been taken.

When reading the text accompanying many path diagrams, one often discovers that although no kind of creature appears in the diagram itself, not just one but several kinds of "organisms" and "units of analysis" have been lurking in the text. In studies of organizations, for example, one may find that one variable comes from observing individuals (perhaps riskiness of decisions made by chief executive officers of companies), another from groups (perhaps productivity of work teams), another from interactions of departments (perhaps amount of information sent or received), another from organizations (perhaps return on investment), and another from collections of organizations (perhaps net balance of trade).

When researchers leap from one kind of living system to another in calculating their correlations, I have no wish to accuse them of either moral turpitude or logical ineptitude. I say only that if they are hoping to capture high correlations, then the method of relative frequencies will dash their hopes. McGrath and Altman showed long ago (1966) that the relations between variables are likely to be stronger when both variables come from individuals, both from groups, or both from organizations, and weaker when one comes from one of those levels of living system and the other comes from another. When you pause to wonder about the populations of people, stimuli, and actions that a study might be sampling when it mixes living systems, the finding of McGrath and Altman is not surprising.

CYCLES

Sometimes authors point out that a person's response, or its effect on some variable, can become in turn an input. You ask me a question (S) and I answer (R). But when I hear my own answer (now S'), I fear it may not convey to you the meaning I want you to get. So I say (R'), "What I mean is. . . . " Authors sometimes speak of that kind of sequence as circular or cyclical. But that conception of cycling is actually still linear. The conception is one of a series of units of S-O-R. The well-known "TOTE unit" of Miller, Galanter, and Pribram (1960) is an example of a conception whose diagram, at first glance, looks as if it might have circular causation in it. But their diagram turns out to be a flow-chart of sequential causation.

Researchers sometimes postulate that two variables affect each other, and they sometimes use a word like "mutually." That "mutual" relation, however, is usually interpreted not as simultaneous causes and effects, but as sequential or alternating. For example, A acting in a trusting manner (X) might cause B to act in a trusting manner (Y), and vice versa. With S-O-R in mind, a researcher might think that comes about because first A acts trustingly, then B thinks it will be safe to act in a trusting manner and does so, then A thinks that showed that his or her trusting act paid off and acts trustingly again, and so forth.

It is also possible to interpret the example of trustbuilding as simultaneous causation. A and B could be working cooperatively on a task that will benefit both, such as sailing a small racing boat that requires simultaneous action by the two people in managing the sails, tending the helm, moving on the deck so as to maintain proper balance, and so on. There trust builds in both persons as the joint action brings success to both. If one waits for the other to show trustworthy action before taking his or her own act, the boat may overturn during the delay. An even more dramatic example is two ice-skating dancers holding hands and whirling with dizzy speed about a point between them. Both perform an act that would be impossible alone, an act possible only through simultaneous joint action. If either waits to see whether trust has paid off, both fall on their ice.

ADDITIVE CORRELATIONAL MODELS

A very common assumption in the use of the method of relative frequencies is that the inputs have a simple additive effect on the output. Outside economics, social scientists almost always sort people by levels of multiple variables by using what statisticians call the "additive model." The general form is $y = a + bx_1 + cx_2 + dx_3 + \ldots + mx_n + e$. The term "$e$" is for error. In that equation, the x's are the inputs and the y is the output. The equation does not permit multiplicative relations among the x's, nor does it permit triggering relations or step-functions. No procedure of multiple correlation, multiple regression, analysis of variance, or the like can detect any of those latter kinds of relation among variables.

If a theory for predicting y is expressed as a linear equation such as the additive model, the equation will produce a single value for y if every one of the x's is given a value, but for any particular value of y there is no unique solution. An infinity of combinations of values of the x's will give that value of y. If we fix x_1, then y can still take on any value whatsoever, depending on the values of the other x's, and an infinity of values is still available. To put it another way, the equation says only that anything can happen. It is no wonder, then, that we must supply the missing restrictions by making assumptions about "error." We collect data, then calculate the correlations between y and each of the x's, and then pretend that in each case the points in the cloud are all really, somehow, on the line $y = a + bx_i$. We then add, in the manner of the additive model, all those equations we got from the correlation calculations. Assuming that y is in every case the same variable, we take, let us say, the equations

$$y = a + bx_1$$

$$y = c + dx_2$$

$$y = f + gx_3$$

and add them together:

$$3y = a + c + f + bx_1 + dx_2 + gx_3.$$

Then relabeling the constants to make things prettier, we have the single equation

$$y = a + bx_1 + cx_2 + dx_3$$

or the additive model.

That is not the only way one can go about things. If we start out instead with a theory that postulates a line or curve, not just a nonrandom scatter of points, the theory must include restrictions on the values of the x's. We put on restrictions by using a theory that can give us more than the one equation of the additive model. We need, indeed, as many independent equations as there are x's. To plot a line in three-dimensional space, for example, suppose our theory allows us to write not only

$y = 1 + 2x_1 + 3x_2$ but also

$y = 2 + 3x_1 + 4x_2.$

Solving those equations simultaneously, we get

$y = -2 - x_1$ and

$y = -1 + x_2.$

If the behavior y is described in various circumstances by the first two equations, then the only conditions under which both of those constraints can hold true at the same time are described by the last two equations. If the behavior y is constrained by both the first two equations, then the last two tell us the value of y we should see for every value of x_1, and similarly for every value of x_2. Our theory is supported when we test it with data if our values for y deviate from the predictions no more than we would expect from the imprecisions of our measuring instruments. Such a theory does not permit deviations due to "unknown variables."

The additive model and all the statistical paraphernalia based on it assume linear causation. Specifying independent equations, as I did above, does not. If human functioning is not linear and sequential, then the linear model and all its corollaries are irrelevant. Few theories in social science, however, begin with sufficient restrictions on the x's. In the next chapter, under "Simultaneity versus Iteration," I will show the kind of absurdity to which the omission of sufficient restriction can lead. In Chapter 11, I will describe some experiments in which the restrictions are sufficient to yield exact predictions.

In explaining about adding equations, I said, "Assuming that y is in every case the same variable." But that is one more dubious assumption. In Chapter 5, I quoted Winne (1983) to the effect that analyses based on the additive model can themselves change y from one variable to another. D. J. Brown (1975), too, has complained that researchers put too much trust in the additive model. He calls it the "linear model," using "linear" as mathematicians do to indicate that the variables in the equation have no powers higher than one and are only added to one another, not multiplied. Brown described six common misuses, some of which were similar to points I have made here. He also assessed the success of the linear model. He counted up the articles reporting Pearson correlations in the *American Educational Research Journal* from 1970, vol. 7, no. 1 through 1974, vol. 11, no. 2. The percentages per year of articles reporting correlations ranged from 38 to 67. The percentage of correlations larger (positive or negative) than .90 was a mere 2. The mean size (positive or negative) of the two-variable correlations in those articles was .27. Furthermore, when Brown calculated the mean of all the coefficients of *multiple* determination (that is, fine slicing), it turned out to be only .24!

STIMULI AND TRAITS

Attributing motivation to personality traits and other internal predispositions fits into the idea of linear causation as well as does attributing motivation to prodding by stimuli. Both ideas fit the input-output scheme. Psychologists do not treat traits as inputs to the organism from outside, of course, but as inputs to the linear process by which input gets converted into output. The idea is analogous to the assembly line, in which materials enter at one end, are reshaped and transformed by various operations at various work stations, and emerge in altered form as products at the other end. Most theories postulate that traits operate at various stations, so to speak, inside the organism, to put shape on the eventual action product. Traits are conceived as motivations in the sense that, when certain input "materials" come along, a trait can add to the processing an instruction of no action, some action, or a great burst of action.

SUMMARY

Certain assumptions lying at the juncture between theory and method appear repeatedly in great reaches of social science investigations. The assumptions of linear causation and of the *S-O-R* typically characterize applications of the method of relative frequencies that go beyond casting a net to the causes of human behavior. The following assumptions seem to me to be part and parcel of the assumption of linear causation: that cause comes before effect, that sequences of cause and effect have ascertainable beginnings and endings, and that the laws of nature are everywhere the same. The first two assumptions are not necessary for casting nets, cumulating catalogs, or writing histories. They are commonly made, however, when researchers interpret causal experiments and correlations.

Those assumptions are far-reaching; they put strong shape on designs and studies. Indeed, many researchers accept those assumptions, when they think about them at all, not as arbitrary assumptions chosen for convenience, but as factual descriptions of the nature of the world we live in. But the assumption of linear causation itself, though it has served physicists well, is not the only assumption about causation available to social scientists. Indeed, the assumption of linear causation leads to experimental designs that actually guarantee faulty inferences about causation, as I showed in Chapter 4 and will show in another way in Chapter 9.

The additive model of relations among multiple variables, so commonly used as part of the method of relative frequencies, makes numerous assumptions that can only sometimes properly describe behavior. Even when all those assumptions match the situation and the subjects, the additive model cannot by itself predict behavior, no matter how good the theory at picking variables nor how good the measurement, because more than one equation is needed to solve for y when there is more than one x.

9

Specimens and Circular Causation

The key idea in circular causation is that internal causes and causes from the environment operate simultaneously, not sequentially, not in tandem or in episodes. The internal operations affect what will be perceived from the environment, and what is perceived affects what is done internally, and all that goes on continuously and seamlessly.

Circular causaton implies a boundary separating the internal from the external, and that separation implies that the internal thing has characteristics that make it in some way a unitary thing with a characteristic way of functioning. It must be, as philosophers say, a *natural kind*. In the next chapter, Figure 10.2 will show circular causation diagrammatically. There, however, circular causation will be mentioned only as a feature of a theory; here, I will argue the necessity of the concept.

Some of the features of the functioning of the human creature are the same in every member of humankind. All of the visible surface features of humans vary from person to person, and all of the visible actions of humans vary from moment to moment and person to person, but my claim is that when we look deeply enough into purposes and patterns, we will find some features of internal functioning that are the same in all of us. If that were not so, we could not transmit our humanness through genes. Furthermore, we can maintain our physical and operational integrity, in our constantly changing environment, only through the lively and immediate responsiveness that comes from making use of circular causation.

How is it that a human can maintain its physical and operational integrity, its rcognizability, its purposes, its anticipated and reliable interactions with the physical world and with others of its kind—all those phenomena we think of as relatively stable—when, because the environmental conditions are never precisely the same, its actions can never be precisely the same? That is the kind of question that cries out for the examination of specimens.

SPECIMENS

For a great many purposes, one or a few specimens of humankind are enough to tell us what to expect from the rest. Morphology, for example. I do not think anyone has ever wanted to take a random sample to estimate the proportion of the population of humans having head, torso, arms, and legs. And once we have seen a few naked members of one sex, we know what to expect from the rest even though all of us encounter only small and nonrandom samples. We do come in some variations. Some of us are male, some female. Some of us are right-handed, some left-handed. Some of us are color-blind, some tone-deaf. None of those variations, however, weakens my argument here.

In regard to the manner of functioning of sensory organs and motor nerves, we all assume that one specimen (or a few to make sure we are not examining an abnormal case) is enough to teach us about all. I do not think even the most devoted believer in the power of nurture over nature will claim that the Munsell color solid is a product of socialization.

When we get to the reaches of the brain that deal with choices of action, perceptions of relationships and categories, formation of principles, and conceptions of the world around us, many people believe that we function with no necessary similarity whatever from person to person. They seem to believe that the structure of those parts of the brain is like the structure of modeling clay— that the brain will take any "shape" impressed upon it from outside. We speak of a person being impressionable. That view is common among both professional and lay psychologists.

There can certainly be no doubt that every one of us, in our more complex mental functioning, is unique, nor that our differing experiences make their contributions to our uniqueness. The place to look for sameness between humans is not in the contents of their beliefs or in the choices they make of objects or people, but in the fact that *all of us do form beliefs* and that *all of us do choose objects and people to act upon.* We can look for the consequences for the person of holding certain beliefs and making choices among objects and people. I shall argue in the next chapter that the consequences are always those of maintaining preferred perceptions. The crucial similarity among us all is that of acting to maintain prferred perceptions and organizing those preferences hierarchically.

I cannot doubt that in some functions, processes, or ways we arrange our interaction with the external world (I admit that those are all vague words at this point), our brains are identical topologically. If it were not so, investigating the nature of humans would be like investigating the nature of the junk in the junk box I described in Chapter 3.

INVARIANTS

The method of specimens is the method of choice of psychophysicists, physiological psychologists, neurologists, and the like. Their journals are full of examples, of which three must suffice.

The Gestalt

The Gestalt tradition, once much more active than it is today, began about 75 years ago with the work of Max Wertheimer, Kurt Koffka, and Wolfgang Köhler. They studied the perception of configuration, transition, and relationship. They soon listed the Gestalt principles of proximity, similarity, symmetry, good continuation, common fate, closure, and figure-and-ground. Here is an example of proximity:

Objectively, there are simply ten things there. But because they are closer together horizontally than vertically (or you might also say that they have better "continuation" horizontally than vertically), we all see two horizontal rows of things—*all* of us. Here is an example of similarity:

o   X   o   X   o

o   X   o   X   o

o   X   o   X   o

There, because of the similar shapes running vertically (and some difference in proximity helps, too), we all see five vertical columns—all of us.

As far as I know, the Gestalt principles worked at the levels of perceived configuration, transition, and relationship for every human creature, every time. I have performed a few of the experiments with students, and they always worked for every person, not merely for some of them. I think it is sad that the Gestalt tradition faded out.

Figure 9.1
Individual Loudness Functions For 11 Subjects

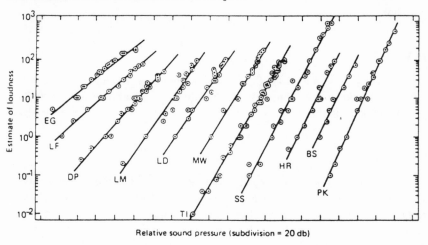

Source: Stevens and Guirao (1964).

Psychophysics

Figure 9.1 shows perceptions of loudness by eleven persons—loudnesses of sounds producing various physical pressures in the air. The figure is Dember and Warm's (1979, p. 100) figure 4.13 taken from Stevens and Guirao (1964). The vertical scale is perceived loudness; the horizontal scale is amplitude of the physical sound waves. The points clustered along one line show the relations perceived by one person. Every circled point on the graph represents one observation of one subject's auditory perception.

Figure 9.1 demonstrates a test of the power law, which connects the perceived (conscious, reportable) magnitude of sensory experience with physical energies, especially when assessed by Stevens's methods of magnitude estimation and production. That is,

$$P = kM^m$$

where P is the perceived magnitude, M is the physical magnitude, m is the exponent or power, and k adjusts for the units used. The equation itself is the invariant. P and M are what the law is about, and m characterizes the individual. The law fits all the sensory modalities that had been investigated by the time Dember and Warm (1979) were writing.

For the psychophysicist, it is not sufficient for the data to fit a statistically significant number of individuals; the data must fit everyone. And they do fit everyone in Figure 9.1.

You can see that the individuals in Figure 9.1 did not agree on the loudness of a particular physical sound pressure. But they all changed their perceptions of loudness, according to the same rule, as the sound pressure changed. Every subject had a line of a particular slope on which the points fell that related sound pressure to loudness, but every line could be generated by the power law.

Figure 9.1 exhibits a hierarchy in perception. If you look only at the points, you see a lot of differences. Each individual reports some sound pressures to be louder than others. One person reports a particular sound pressure to be louder than another person does. Furthermore, individuals differ in the changes of loudness they perceive: the slopes of the lines differ. We find no invariances in those comparisons (intensity and sensation) of loudness. When we look, however, at the configuration of points for any single individual, we see that the points array themselves in a straight line (against the logarithmic scale)—given some small errors of measurement. That is an invariant within the individual. The invariant across individuals is the power law itself, which has the same form for every individual: $P = kM^m$.

Complexity

For millennia, people have noticed that we seem almost always to pay attention to something unusual, novel—to something ornate instead of plain, spicy instead of bland, full of detail instead of simple. People often seem to act out of pure curiosity, to explore new places, things, or activities just for the pleasure of it.

Dember, Earl, and Paradise (1957) thought of the attraction of a more interesting piece of environment as its "stimulus complexity." Their study is also recounted by Dember and Warm (1979, pp. 397-98). Dember, Earl, and Paradise built two circular runways for rats, with the two circles overlapping so that the whole assembly formed a fat figure-eight. A rat placed at the juncture could choose to wander in either circle and was free to change circles at will. The researchers carried out two experiments with this apparatus. In the second experiment, the walls of one circle were painted with black and white horizontal stripes; the walls of the other were in some series of trials uniformly white and in others uniformly black. The researchers postulated the striped circle to be more complex to the rats than the plain circle.

For five days, the researchers put 16 rats into the apparatus, each for 60 minutes per day. They watched the rats continuously and recorded the time each rat spent in one circle or the other. Few rats spent the whole 60 minutes in one circle, but every rat spent a preponderance of time in one circle rather than the other. On the first day, eight of the 16 rats "preferred" the more complex (striped) circle. On the second day, all eight maintained their preference, and four more rats came to prefer the more complex circle. On the third day, the remaining four did so. *All* rats maintained that preference during the remaining trials. *No* rat, once having come to prefer the striped circle, ever reverted to a preference for the plain one. That outcome was exactly what the experimenters had predicted.

The theory proposed by Dember and Earl (1957) was not simply that creatures always pay more attention to experience perceived as more complex. Rather, they said, we pay more attention to those features of the environment that can give us more information than we have now, but not too much more. After we become familiar with a place, a picture, a piece of music, someone's style of conversation, we become ready to look away from it toward more complex things. As we learn how to work one kind of problem in mathematics successfully, we become more attracted to a kind of problem that offers more difficulty. Dember and Earl put the name *pacer stimulus* on the degree of complexity that we are ready to put behind us as we turn our attention to greater complexity. The degree of complexity to which we will pay most attention is a degree not too far beyond the pacer stimulus; too much complexity is confusing, even frightening.

The invariant here is the movement from less comlex to more. Individuals (rats or humans) vary in the time they take to get ready for the next degree of complexity. The level of complexity sought next varies with the person, the embedding environment, the person's task or purpose, sometimes the person's degree of fatigue, and so on. Within all those influences, however, the focus on the range just beyond the pacer stimulus remains. We might call it the effect of familiarity, mastery, information absorption, or any of a dozen other words that point to "getting something under one's belt" and going on to the next interesting thing. Van de Rijt-Plooij (1986) has published some evidence that I interpret to mean that chimpanzee mothers, in rearing their young, understand the pacer stimulus very well.

Dember, Earl, and Paradise used no control group. They did not put a "treatment" upon the rats at a time chosen for their own convenience, with the expectation that the rats would respond to it at that convenient time. They substituted no rat for any other, physically or in logic. (Because they observed every rat individually and examined the data from every rat, they could point to any rat and say, "There is a rat that did what we predicted.") The causation was not conceived as a stimulus event causing a particular act. The experimenters did not expect the striped runway to cause the rats to run immediately into it and stay there. Indeed, no rat did that.

The idea of the experimenters, clearly, was to examine how the rats dealt with their environment to maintain a preferred perception. Every rat was observed continuously so that the experimenters could discover how each individual rat chose its own acts at its own moments. The prediction was simply that a rat would not choose behavior that violated the idea of the advancing pacer stimulus.

I hope those examples will suffice to show what I mean by invariants. The conception of the invariant in the method of specimens is very different from that in the method of relative frequencies. In the *S-O-R*, the thing you hope to count on happening is the response. You hope to predict an act: pressing a lever, turning right in a maze, answering a question "yes," choosing to read one kind of article about intelligence tests rather than another, quitting a job, divorcing a spouse. In the method of specimens, you do not expect the creature to deliver a particular act (such as reporting a particular loudness) or to behave according to some outcome presumably associated with a particular stimulus, but rather to behave according to its own nature, and you hunt for the regularities in that nature. Look again at Figure 9.1. It is not the nature of humans to say, "That's very loud," when they hear a tone of a certain physical magnitude. Some will say it is very loud, some will say it is not. It is the nature of every human, however, to perceive the relative loudness of one sound in comparison to another in proportion to a power of the physical magnitudes of the two sounds.

NATURAL KINDS

In recent years, the idea of "natural kinds" has come into currency among philosophers of science; by 1977, enough philosophers had written on the topic that Stephen P. Schwartz published an anthology. But even in 1967, Schlesinger said boldly, "Scientists consider an individual object as a member of some natural kind or do not consider it at all."

A natural kind, I gather, is an object or a piece of stuff that can be recognized by the invariants in its behavior, regardless of the label or classification to which some of us have become accustomed. Iron pyrites is not gold. A whale is not a fish. Hydrogen is a natural kind. So are a paramecium, an aardvark, and a human. A species is a natural kind. Maybe life is a natural kind. Some people act as if human groups and organizations are natural kinds. I will comment on that belief in Chapter 12.

Psychologists and other social scientists are, I think, almost as prone to reification as anybody else. If I read the philosophers correctly, they are telling us that form, shape, temperature, and velocity cannot be natural kinds. A natural kind can be recognized by its behavior, but behavior itself is not a natural kind. Specific heat may be a character by which we can tell a natural kind, but rate of heating is not a natural kind; it is a variable. The preference for moving over the ground by walking on the hind legs may be one of the characters by which we can tell a natural kind, but the frequency of doing so is not; it is a variable.

A variable—behavior that an individual can show in one or another degree—is not a natural kind. Aggressiveness, introversion, skill, schizophrenia, and delinquency are not natural kinds. I do not think that carpenters, juvenile delinquents, or leaders of corporations are natural kinds. Nothing is wrong with making a specialty of studying skeletons, or hearts, or language, or aggression, but there is a great deal wrong with ignoring the ways the whole creature makes use of skeleton, heart, language, or aggression to carry out the purposes of the whole creature. Organs and actions serve purposes. I will say more about that in the next chapter.

CIRCULAR CAUSATION

The physicists gave us the idea of the *field*, first put into mathematics by James Clerk Maxwell in the middle of the last century. In a field, every infinitesimal point is interdependent with, in tension with, every other. Think of a stretched rubber sheet, or think of a sphere like a rubber balloon. When you push on a rubber balloon with your finger, every part of the balloon is immediately deformed to some extent. Every part immediately alters its tension. What happens under your finger, furthermore, depends not only on the rubber at the locality of your finger, but on every part of the spherical rubber sheet. If someone else happens to be poking at another part of the balloon, that affects the deformation at your finger.

Pulses transmitted across synapses in a series of neurons are of course much slower than an electric pulse in a wire. Despite the slow speed of a neural pulse, I find it useful to think of a feedback loop in the neural net as a field instead of a series of discreet "messages." Loops are not composed of strings of single neurons, but of bundles of many neurons. The effect of the electrochemical action in the bundles is like that of a current, not like that of a pulse. Action in the neural loop is not like a ball rolling around a track. It is more like an entire circle of balls, all touching. When one moves, they all move. The electrochemical neural current, like the purely electrical one, acts to maintain a potential, with the potential at every point simultaneously interdependent with that at every other.

CAUSE AND EFFECT

Imagine a flag flying in the breeze. It is easy to think of the breeze causing the flag to rise and fall, wave and flutter. When, however, air currents press against the flag, some of the air is deflected and slowed, giving up energy to the work of lifting the flag or of whipping it side to side. The mass of the flag causes the air currents to change their velocity (speed and direction), and the breeze on the lee side of the flag has a different character and, overall, a lower amount of energy than the breeze on the windward side.

At the interface between the flag and the breeze, flag, air, and earth all act together through mass, movement, and gravity in a continuing dynamic interaction. We like to say, when the flag lifts, that the air is pushing it up. We like to say, when the flag falls, that it is sinking through the air—pushing the air out of its way. But the air is pushing at every moment, and the flag is pushing at every moment. We see the flag change its position because air and flag exchange energy. Everything happens simultaneously.

The sequence of cause and effect remains a mystery to me. We might ask, for example, which gets there first—gravitation or bodies? Neither. Gravitation is our name for the way bodies act in space. Here are a couple of remarks from Geza Szamosi's (1986) fascinating book on time and space:

> If you place a body somewhere in space, then *the mass of that body influences the structure of . . . spacetime.* (p. 173)

> There is no gravitational attraction between the sun and the planets. The only role of the sun is to change the structure of spacetime. In this spacetime structure, the planets experience no force at all. They move like free bodies . . . because of the presence of the sun, the free motion . . . does not go on a straight line, but on a more general curve. (p. 175)

To make the simultaneous interaction more clear, Szamosi quotes, in a footnote on page 175, a textbook by Misner, Thorne, and Wheeler: "Space tells matter how to move," and "Matter tells space how to curve."

I do not think the matter of cause and effect is as simple as it seems when you are pounding a nail with a hammer. I think it deserves more thought than most of us social scientists give it. But this is not the place for an extended disquisition on the topic. What my puzzling comes down to, in my mind, is that it takes some time for currents to traverse the neural loop, but it happens so fast in comparison to the speed with which muscles can act that for all practical purposes I prefer to think of causation in the feedback loop as circular and simultaneous.

SIMULTANEITY VERSUS ITERATION

Finally, I will point out the effect of this point of view on model building. When you want to build a model in a computer that will act like a living creature, taking action in the loop as being simultaneous or taking it as iteratively cycling makes a great difference.

Suppose we have collected some data from observing a person standing with an umbrella in a blowing rain. For simplicity of discussion, let us suppose that the density of the rain and the force of the wind remain constant while only the direction of the wind varies, changing from one point of the compass to another as the person stands there trying to keep the amount of rain in the face to some preferred small amount.

Let $Y =$ amount of rain in the face per unit of time.

$X =$ compass direction toward which the umbrella is pointing.

$W =$ compass direction from which the wind is coming.

$Y^* =$ preferred amount of rain in the face.

$D =$ action of the person, the angular change the person gives to the umbrella.

Then $X - W =$ angle of the umbrella relative to the wind.

$Y^* - Y =$ difference between the amount of rain striking the face and the amount the person prefers, expressed here for later algebraic convenience as the shortfall of received rain below the amount the person prefers.

The first statement of our theory is one about the sheer physics of the situation, a statement that the amount of rain in the face depends on the angle of the umbrella relative to the wind:

$$Y = a(X - W) \tag{1}$$

The second statement postulates the action of the person in response to the difference between preferred and received rain:

$$D = j(Y^* - Y) \tag{2}$$

The third statement connects the physical outcome, the angle of the umbrella X, to the angular action or effort D of the person:

$$X = kD \tag{3}$$

I will explain later about a, j, and k.

The three equations tell us the relations among variables that would have to be built into a model of this behavior and the constants that would have to be evaluated. Let us now solve the three equations simultaneously for X and Y. We will discover that both the amount of rain in the face Y and the angle to which the umbrella is brought X depend on both an *internal* quantity, the preferred amount of rain in the face Y^*, and an *external* quantity, the direction of the wind W. To solve for Y, we substitute the right-hand side of equation (2) into equation (3) and get:

$$X = jk(Y^* - Y) \tag{4}$$

Then substituting the right side of (4) into (1), we have:

$$Y = a[jk(Y^* - Y) - W]$$

and simplifying that, we arrive at

$$Y = \frac{ajkY^* - aW}{1 + ajk}. \tag{5}$$

Now, to solve for X, we go back to (4) and substitute into it the right-hand side of (1), giving

$$X = jk[Y^* - a(X - W)] \tag{6}$$

and simplifying that, we arrive at

$$X = \frac{jkY^* + ajkW}{1 + ajk}. \tag{7}$$

Simultaneity

Equation (5) tells us that the amount of rain Y the person gets in the face depends on the amount the person prefers Y^*, the direction of the wind W, and some constants that I will explain shortly. That is, the actual amount of rain in the face is a joint result of the disturbance function (the direction of the wind W) and the preferred perception Y^*. The internal standard Y^*, acting in comparison with the incoming perception, determines the person's action that will oppose the effect of W. This theory requires, I repeat, that the result of the interaction of the person with the environment be a joint function of a quantity inside the person and a quantity outside.

Equation (7) tells us that the moving angle of the umbrella X also depends on Y^* and W, and depends as well, but in a way somewhat different from equation (5), on the constants. The two equations (5) and (7) specify the relations among variables that would have to be built into a working model of the behavior with the umbrella. The two equations apply to every single individual, not to averages over individuals.

This model is not built on linear causation. The input perception of rain on the face does not produce one particular act. You cannot even say that a certain amount of rain on a certain part of the face produces a certain amount of arm motion. The amount of arm motion will depend on how fast the wind direction is changing, including sudden reversals of direction. But it is more correct to think of the output not as arm motion, but as muscle tension, and that will vary even though the arm motion is the same, because of the changing tensions needed to move the umbrella to a particular position as the shifting wind presses upon it.

The arm motion is not a series of distinguishable acts. The motion is continuous until the rain in the face reaches the minimum. Then the muscles reverse against the inertia of the arms and umbrella to stop the motion. But the muscles do not then stop working. They now act to hold the umbrella in place and the rain in the face to a minimum. The change in arm position is now zero and so is the rate of change, and the muscles are working to maintain that state. The number zero is as good a quantity as any other as far as the muscles know anything about the matter, and that zero motion maintains the minimum rain in the face the persons wants. Action is continuous, and the causations between X and Y are circular, not sequential.

To build an actual model, it is not enough to work out the general forms of the equations. We must also find values for the constants. In equation (1), the constant a tells us the proportionality between the amount of rain in the face Y and the relative angle of the umbrella $(X - W)$; that is, a is the number of units of rain in the face generated by one unit of relative umbrella angle. The constant a serves to convert units of angle into units of rain, but it also summarizes the physical constants in the situation (or factors that we are taking as constant for the purpose of this example) such as the density of the rain, the force of the wind, and the diameter of the umbrella. Arbitrarily, for this hypothetical example, let us set $a = 2$.

In equation (2), the constant j is the sensitivity of the person to the error $(Y^* - Y)$. The constant j tells us the number of units of angle the person will move the umbrella for one unit of discrepancy between rain in the face desired and received. Let us set $j = 50$, a moderate sensitivity in living creatures.

In equation (3), the constant k tells us the number of units of actual umbrella angle X that will be produced by one unit of movement or effort D on the part of the person. This is merely a matter of units of measurement. Equation (3) says that X is the same as D except for units of measurement. Let $k = 2$.

Now let us see what equations (5) and (7) look like when we fill in the numbers. For Y, we have

$$Y = \frac{(2)(50)(2)Y^* - (2)W}{1 + (2)(50)(2)} = 0.995Y^* - 0.010W \tag{8}$$

and for X, we have

$$X = \frac{(50)(2)Y^* + (2)(50)(2)W}{1 + (2)(50)(2)} = 0.498Y^* + 0.995W \tag{9}$$

Now let us see how those specifications would work for a person whose preference for rain in the face is $Y^* = 1$ at a moment when the wind angle is $W = 15$. Substituting those values into (8), we find our model telling us that the amount of rain the person would get in the face is

$$Y = (0.995)(1) - (0.010)(15) = 0.845.$$

The value of 0.845 is 0.155 units away from the preferred value of 1.0. When we remember that one unit of umbrella angle generates 2 units of rain in the face, a discrepancy of 0.155 seems to be pretty good control of rain in the face. Now, substituting $Y^* = 1$ and $W = 15$ into (9), we get the compass direction of the umbrella:

$$X = (0.498)(1) + (0.995)(15) = 15.423.$$

The discrepancy of 0.423 between the wind angle (15) and the umbrella angle allows the person to receive 0.845 units of rain in the face.

Now, to explore the functioning of the model a little, let us see what it would predict for a person whose preference for rain in the face is $Y^* = 20$ units. The model is required to work right not just for people who have the same preference, but for anybody, regardless of preference. People are not alike in their preferences, but in their dogged insistence on satisfying them. Our model should doggedly do that, too. Substituting $Y^* = 20$ in (8) and (9) and keeping $W = 15$, we get $Y = 19.750$ and $X = 24.885$. For a preference of 20 and the same constants, the model controls the rain in the face to 0.250 units of the desired amount by an umbrella angle 4.885 units away from the wind.

To explore a little more, let us increase the sensititivy j. Let $j = 150$, with $a = 2$, $k = 2$, $W = 15$, and $Y^* = 1$, as in the first example. We find now that $Y = 0.948$ and $X = 15.474$. In the first example, with $j = 50$, the angle of the umbrella (X) departed 0.423 units from the direction of the wind. Now, with $j = 150$, the departure is 0.474. The small increase of 0.051 in departure brings the amount of rain in the face (Y) to 0.948, a large improvement over the earlier value of 0.845. With $j = 50$, the amount of rain in the face was 0.155 short of the desired 1.0. With $j = 150$, the amount is only 0.052 short.

Those few explorations of the model show well enough that the model behaves very much the way humans behave with umbrellas. The theory requires that values be ascertained for a, j, k, Y^*, and W. The values of a and W could be measured directly—if the wind were constant. The other values could be estimated in preliminary runs. Later runs would then test the theory quantitatively for every individual.

Iterating

In the foregoing demonstration, we solved the system equations simultaneously; we required the relations among variables all to hold simultaneously. Let us now pretend the causation is linear, that the feedback loop acts in a series of iterations, that the person positions the umbrella through a sequence of *S-O-R* cyclings. To do that, we will use the system equations iteratively instead of simultaneously. We will suppose that in the first *S-O-R* sequence, a splat of rain in the face causes a motion of the umbrella. In the second, the motion of the umbrella causes a cessation of the rain in the face, and so on.

We go back to the system equations (1), (2), and (3). As (1) we had

$$Y = a(X - W) \tag{1}$$

and from (2) and (3) we had

$$X = jk(Y^* - Y). \tag{4}$$

Let $a=2$, $j=50$, $k=2$, $Y^*=1$, and $W=15$. Then we have

$Y = 2(X - 15)$ or

$Y = 2X - 30$ (10)

and

$X = (50)(2)(1 - Y)$ or

$X = 100 - 100Y$ (11)

Let us begin with equation (11) and, arbitrarily, with no rain in the face; that is, let $Y=0$. Then we would have

$X = 100 - 100Y$, and since $Y=0$,

$X = 100$.

Now, turning for the second *S-O-R* to equation (10), let us see how much rain in the face a value of $X = 100$ brings us:

$Y = 2X - 30$, and substituting the value of $X = 100$ from the first S-O-R,

$Y = (2)(100) - 30 = 170$.

Those values for X and Y are nothing like the values we got from the simultaneous solution. Will the values of X and Y converge on the simultaneous values? For the third S-O-R, substitute 170 for Y in the equation for X:

$X = 100 - 100Y = 100 - (100)(170) = -16,900$.

For the fourth S-O-R:

$Y = 2X - 30 = (2)(-16,900) - 30 = -33,830$.

The fifth *S-O-R* would give $X = +3,383,100$, and the sixth $Y = +6,766,170$. We are getting a new value of the angle X at every iteration, a rapidly increasing and oscillating one, and a similarly increasing oscillation for Y. The iterative prediction is that the person would make increasingly wide swings with the umbrella until the person would be whirling like a dervish. Clearly, the interative interpretation leads to nonsense. Nobody can keep rain off the face with a feedback loop in which the parts take turns acting. Causes in the feedback loop are simultaneous.

SUMMARY

Investigating a living creature, a natural kind, requires a method different from investigating a junk box. The method of specimens looks for the invariants to be found within individuals and among individuals.

The method of specimens is alive and well. It has always been used by some researchers in psychophysics and similar disciplines. It was the method of choice in Gestalt psychology. It has had signal successes in studies of perception. In Chapters 10 and 11, I will show its coupling with a general theory of the functioning of living creatures.

The idea of causation is not a simple one. But if you treat internal and external causes as going on simultaneously and think of the internal processing of those causes as circular, you get predictions that mirror actual behavior. If you treat the processing as iterative, you do not.

The method of relative frequencies will tell you the proportion of people in a sample who hold off specified amounts of rain. It will tell you those proportions among people who say, ''I don't like rain in the face,'' ''I like a little rain in the face,'' and so on. It will tell you the proportions of people who say those things while waiting for a bus, while sitting on the sand at the shore, and so on. It will not tell you how any of those people can be capable of keeping rain out of their faces. The method of specimens can tell you whether the person has any internal standard at all about rain in the face, and it can enable you to write specifications for a model that acts the way individuals with umbrellas act.

IV

What the Method of Specimens Will Do

In Parts I and II, I wrote about what the method of relative frequencies can and cannot do. It can locate densities of kinds of behavior. It cannot find out how a specimen of humankind functions—the rules by which it interacts with its environment. In Part III, I explained why I think circular causation, not linear causation, must provide the metatheory for the study of specimens.

In Chapter 10 of Part IV, I will describe a theory suitable for the study of specimens—a theory that rests on circular causation and the postulate that we act to control our *perceptions*. In Chapter 11, I will recount a few experiments that demonstrate how very well that theory serves to discover invariances. In Chapter 12, I will set forth some implications of the theory for social psychology.

10

Control Theory

I have been lucky enough to come upon a theory and a growing body of experimentation that shows brilliantly what can be done with a theory firmly melded with the method of specimens. The theory is called "control theory" and is credited primarily to William T. Powers. I will cite his writings later.

CONTROL AS FACT

Theory arises to explain observed facts. Control theory begins with the observation of behavior as control—that is, the observation that living creatures act to control what happens to them, that one of the consequences of any action is always the control of some energy the creature can sense. Examples abound. When you drive along a highway, you control the position of the car between the painted lines—a position you sense with your eyes. When you draw a horizontal line across a page, you control the distance you see between the line and the top or bottom edge of the paper. When you walk, you control the upright position of your body—a position you sense with your semicircular canals. When you take a sip of tea, you control the distance between cup and lip. As I type these words, I control the direction, momentum, and distance of the movements that I feel with my fingers.

Our bodies maintain their internal temperature within a very small range. We often act on the environment to aid our bodies in doing that. To feel warmer, we put on more clothing, go into heated buildings, eat more food, and so on.

To feel cooler, we remove clothing, stand in a breeze, go into cooled buildings, drink cold water, and so on. We act, in other words, to control the sensation of heat flow in or out of our bodies. We act to bring the heat flow into proper balance with the internal production of heat; we act to *control* the sensing of heat flow, not necessarily to maximize it or minimize it. The acts people choose in order to maintain internal temperature are not invariant; that they will act to do it, all of them, is an invariant.

The Illusion of Output Control

Behavior may look like the output response in the *S-O-R* if you fail to notice the effect contributed by the environment. Then it is easy to think that the person produced the act free from any hindrance, that the act came solely from within the person. Driving in a lane on the highway, the driver seems to be steering where he or she wishes. But the driver does not just point the car down the lane and let it go. The driver continues actively to steer, because the wind and the bumps on the road keep changing by a little the direction the car is headed. The position of the car in the lane comes from the *simultaneous interaction* of the environmental disturbances and the driver's corrective steering.

Sometimes we fail to notice the disturbance from the environment because it is invisible—because we, the observers, cannot sense it. Consider walking. As observers, we can see the ground and the movements of the walker's legs and body, but we cannot see the gravity against which the walker is acting. Nevertheless, walking cannot be done in zero gravity. In interaction with the moon's gravity, one-sixth that of the earth, the astronauts could not move in the way we think of as walking. They had to use the "bunny hop." They did not design the bunny hop or "decide" to use it. They simply interacted with the moon's gravity in that way to get where they wanted to go.

We fail to notice disturbances, too, because we cope with most of them very easily. In ordinary circumstances, walking looks graceful and smooth. Drivers with only a little experience can purr along the highway and carry on a spirited conversation at the same time.

The Illusion of Stimulus Control

When an event stands out for us from the other events going on in the environment, and very soon afterward a person starts moving or changes from one kind of action to another, it is easy for us to conclude that the particular event caused, all by itself, the action of the person. The mother calls, "Clarissa, come here!" and the child goes to the mother. It is easy to think that nothing more was necessary to get the child to the mother than the mother's call.

If you slap at a person's face, the person is very likely to dodge. The dodging seems obviously to be a response to the stimulus of the slapping motion. But the environmental event is not the sole determiner of the action. What happens depends on what the person wants to control. The dodging person has foremost the purpose of maintaining an unslapped face. Sometimes, however, people do let themselves get slapped, maybe having the purpose of showing how little the act will avail the slapper. The environmental event cannot select the action. The person selects an action that will maintain the feeling (perception) of an unslapped face or the perception of the self as unmoved by the slap. In either case, the person selects an action that will oppose the effect of the environmental disturbance.

The one theory I know that is explicit about circular causation, feedback loops through the environment, internal standards, hierarchies of purpose, and the time required for neural rearrangements and for physical action—all those features and phenomena—and is also able to produce physical, working models that behave like humans quantitatively, not just qualitatively, is the control theory originated mostly by William T. Powers. Like all theorists, Powers has built upon the work of others. But Powers (for example, in 1973b and 1978) tells the story of earlier work himself; I will not take space for it here. I turn now to a brief exposition of Powers's control theory.

THE RUBBER BANDS

I will introduce the theory by describing a simple exercise you might like to try. You could also call it a demonstration, game, or experiment. I borrow it from Powers (1973b, pp. 241-44).

Get two rubber bands three or four inches long. Knot them end to end as shown in Figure 10.1. Enlist a friend. You hook a finger into the end of one rubber band, and your friend hooks a finger into the end of the other. Tell your friend something like, "You are the experimenter. Move your finger as you like. Watch what I do. When you can explain what is causing me to do what I do, let me know."

When you set out to do this little game, you will be accepting some internal standards from me, the author of this book. When you get the rubber bands, you will be trying to match your perception of what you see yourself doing to the internal image you formed when you read the words "two rubber bands three or four inches long." Humans borrow standards from one another by the dozens, every day. Please pass the butter. Drive on the right-hand side. Stand

Figure 10.1
Knotted Rubber Bands

in line. Read English from left to right and down. When your friend accepts your instructions for the game, your friend will be adopting some internal standards from you.

When you sit down with your friend, place yourself so that the knot joining the rubber bands lies above some inconspicuous mark you can see but is unlikely to draw the attention of your friend—a small scar on a table top, a piece of lint on your knee, or the like. As your friend's finger moves, move yours so that the knot remains stationary over the mark.

Now you have adopted a standard for the position of the knot. When something acts to disturb the position of the knot, you will act to restore the knot to its position over the mark. You will move in any way necessary to do that.

You cannot, of course, keep the knot stationary if your friend moves faster than your natural reaction time can compensate. Some people playing this game seem to want to move jerkily, too fast. If that happens, ask your friend to slow down. The lessons to be learned will be much more obvious to both of you if you are able to keep the knot continuously over the mark. You might say, "Don't move so fast I can't keep up."

Your friend will notice before long that every motion of her finger is reflected exactly by a motion of yours. When she pulls back, you pull back. When she moves inward, you move inward. When she circles to her left, you circle to your left. You must do that, of course, to keep the knot stationary. Your action illustrates very plainly the phenomenon of control—that we act in opposition to a disturbance.

Notice that you perform many different acts to maintain your perception of the knot remaining over the mark. You move your finger to the left, to the right, forward, backward, diagonally at varying speeds.

Most people, when they announce that they have solved the puzzle, will say that you are simply imitating what they do, or mirroring it, or words to that effect. Some will put it more forcefully: that whatever they do, you are acting in opposition to it. Almost all will say or imply that *they* are the cause of your behavior. A few people will notice that the knot remains stationary, but most will not. Most will say that your intent is to do something in reaction to *them*. But then you deny that. Those who do not notice the stationary knot will eventually give up and ask, "All right, what *is* causing your behavior?" Then you explain that you have merely been keeping the knot over the mark.

No, you tell your friend, your purpose has not been to oppose any intention of hers. Your purpose has not been to frustrate her. If, instead of her finger, a machine had been hooked to the rubber band, you would have moved as you did. Your purpose was to keep the knot motionless over the mark; that's all. You moved to oppose any motion of the knot away from the mark, not to oppose *her*. Your motivation had nothing to do with what your friend might have been trying to do; you did not care. You watched only the knot and the mark.

Reactions of "experimenters" will vary widely. A few will accuse you of sophistry and go away grumbling. Most will be surprised, even dumbfounded, to have missed the obvious. A few will find so many of their previous ideas so wrenched and shaken that they will cogitate for days or weeks afterward.

What do we predict here? We do not undertake to predict the reaction of your friend to the game. That is unpredictable. Your friend's reaction is a collection of particular acts. We do not presume to predict particular acts. We do not predict, either, the ways your friend's finger will move. Those, too, are particular acts. We do predict that your friend's finger will hook into the rubber band and move this way and that as long as she accepts the "standard" you have offered her—that of playing the game. At some point, of course, she will give up maintaining that standard and move to a new activity. Perhaps she will turn to discussing psychology with you, or perhaps she will suggest a different game to play.

We do predict, too, the *kind* of motion you will give your finger. We do not predict the particular acts of your finger. We do predict that you will move in whatever way is necessary to restore the knot to its place over the mark—as long as you accept that perception as your internal standard. Obviously, you are not going to keep that standard at the top of your hierarchy for more than a few minutes. You have other things to do with your life.

Notice that you acted to maintain *perceptual* input—to keep unchanged your perception of the knot over the mark. You did not care where your finger went as long as you were successful in maintaining that perception. You moved or did not move as necessary. If the rules of the game had permitted, you might have used many methods other than moving your finger. You might have used words: "Hey, friend, leave the knot where it is." Or you might have got a hammer and nail and nailed the knot in place. You did not act to control output (a particular act) as an end in itself; you did not insist upon taking any one action.

Notice that the game took the shape it did only because you had a purpose. If you had had no purpose, there would have been no game. If you had a different purpose, perhaps to keep the knot moving back and forth along an imaginary line, the pattern of your movements would have been different.

How could you move as you did, controlling the position of the knot? Control theory says you could do it because of a feedback loop. You saw the knot beginning to move. That perception got compared in your mind with a picture of what a knot directly over a mark looks like. The discrepancy between your incoming perception and the reference-picture caused a message to go to your finger telling it to move in a certain direction at a certain rate. Your finger moved. The knot moved back toward the mark. You saw it do so, and that perception went into your brain for comparison with the reference-picture. And so on, round and round. Part of that loop was in your neural net, part in the environment. As long as you maintained your purpose, your internal standard for the position of the knot, that loop had no beginning or ending.

It is impossible to claim that causation in the loop lay only outside you or only inside you. Did your friend's pulling back on her band (and disturbing the knot) cause you to pull back on yours? Yes and no. You would not have needed to pull back on yours if she had not pulled back on hers. But you would not have pulled back, either, if you had not had the purpose of keeping the knot over the mark. Your friend could take her choice of causes. Pulling back on her rubber band, she could say, "Ha! Made you pull back on yours, didn't I?" Or, when you bumped your elbow on the chair back, she could say, "Don't blame me. It was your choice to keep the silly knot over the mark."

The movement of your friend's finger—what might be taken as the "stimulus"—was not invariably followed by a movement of yours. Suppose both of you push your fingers toward each other until the rubber bands become slack. Suppose your friend pushes her finger still more toward you. Because your rubber band is no longer in tension, the knot does not move, and you do not move your finger.

Notice that as long as the rubber bands are taut, there is a perfect correlation between the motions of your friend's finger and of yours—between the stimulus or input and the response or output—but that correlation, by itself, tells your friend or an onlooker *nothing about you.* Your friend or an onlooker learns something about you when he or she finds the thing that is *not* correlated with the stimulus—namely, the unmoving knot. Then the friend or onlooker knows that you have an internal standard and that you are acting according to it to control your perception of the position of the knot. The internal standard is what the friend or onlooker needs to know about to make correct predictions, and to find the internal standard, the friend or onlooker must discover the quantity that is *not* correlated with stimulus or response.

THE LOOP

Now I will get a little more technical, though not much. Figure 10.2 shows the functions I have been talking about and their causal interrelations. I made Figure 10.2 by condensing and simplifying several of Powers's diagrams.

The left portion of the diagram, labeled "Actor," represents the neural net. The right portion, labeled "Environment," represents the part of the world outside the neural net. The large box to the right of the vertical line stands for what we see as control. When we see the fact of control, we see the result of an action that contains some feature (the "feedback function") that opposes some feature (the "disturbance function") of an independent environmental event. We can see events represented at the right side of the figure without having any picture of the left side. We cannot, however, see directly the *features* or *aspects* of the events which, for this person at this moment, constitute the disturbance and the opposition to it.

The left side of the figure represents control theory. That is the part that explains what we see at the right side. I will take you through the whole figure, using the rubber-band game to illustrate. Let's start at the upper right corner.

Figure 10.2
The Loop

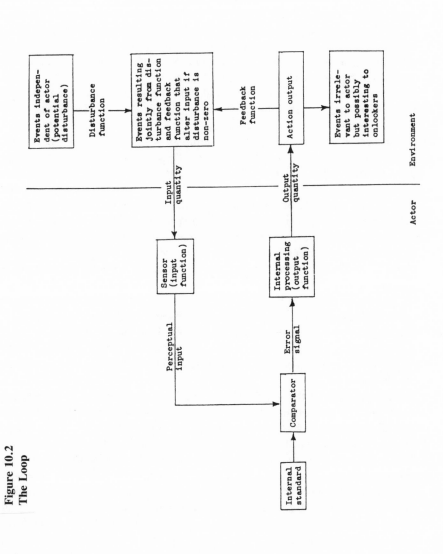

The friend moves the finger. That is an event in the environment independent of anything the actor (the subject we are observing) does. I do not mean that actors are incapable of influencing friends; I mean let's take the case in which the friend acts freely, uninstructed by the actor. In the rubberband game, the "disturbance function" is the series of physical events that convert the movement of the friend's finger into a position of the knot. The "event resulting jointly" is the position of the knot resulting jointly from the movement of the friend's finger and the opposing movement of the actor's finger. The "input quantity" is then the distance and direction of the knot from the mark, a quantity sensed by the sensor—the eye, in this case.

The friend's finger may or may not disturb the actor's input quantity. In the rubber-band game, it does disturb the input quantity—the position of the knot—except when the rubber bands go slack.

The sensor converts the sensed positions of knot and mark in the environment into a neural signal representing a perception. The sensor, in other words, provides the "input function" converting light energy into neural signals. The perception goes to the comparator. And so does the neural signal representing the internal standard, or the internal picture of where the knot *ought* to be. (The internal standard, in this case, is, to speak figuratively, a picture of zero distance from the knot to the mark or perhaps some minimally acceptable distance such as a sixteenth of an inch.) The comparator sends out an "error signal." If the perception matches the standard, the error is zero; otherwise, the error is non-zero.

The error signal goes through some processing in the neural net. It must be converted into signals to muscles to cause them to pull this way and that. Its conversion is affected by a great many memories having to do with visual patterns, magnitudes of effects of muscular effort, the nature of rubber bands, and so on. The conversion of the error signal into the signals to muscles is the "output function."

The movement of the actor's finger is the "output quantity." The "feedback function" is contained in the series of physical events through which the motion of the actor's finger is converted into a position of the knot. The feedback function interacts with the disturbance function, and round we go again.

The action output always produces more effects in the environment than the output quantity relevant to the input quantity the actor is controlling. The actor also watches the knot (by adjusting the head, eyeball, iris, or lens), shifts in the chair, breaths, wriggles the shoulders, maybe exclaims "Ha!" and so on. Those are examples of the irrelevant events mentioned in the box at the lower right. We can never produce a pure output quantity. Sometimes onlookers care about what the actor cares about, sometimes not. One onlooker may want to watch how closely the actor can keep the knot on the mark. Another may be more interested in the conversation that goes on during the game—if any. If you put on a coat to keep warm, some onlooker may care more about whether it is stylish than about whether it is keeping you warm.

That is the loop. You can start at any place in it to trace the sequence of events. It has no beginning or ending. It is not, however, self-contained; it is an open system. It runs in and out of the environment. *The independent disturbing event and the action output are always interacting to produce an input quantity, and the internal standard and the perception are always interacting to produce an output quantity.* That is not to say that every event in the environment disturbs some input quantity, some perception of how things ought to be. Many things happen to which we pay no attention.

A warning about reading Figure 10.2. The lines with the arrows on them do not represent correlations. Nor do they portray a time sequence; many events in the loop occur simultaneously. But I do want the Figure to convey to you more than a vague idea that something happens. Every arrow on the actor's side in Figure 10.2 is meant to represent the flow of actual neural currents in an actual nervous system. A line with an arrow on it does not, of course, stand for one neuron. The diagram is a vast oversimplification. A line with an arrow stands for flows through perhaps millions of neurons and the balancing of hundreds, maybe thousands, of subnetworks in the neural net. Nevertheless, the line with the arrow stands for a neural event, however complex, connecting in the specified order two specified functions—which are, in turn, also neural events. On the side of the environment, a line with an arrow also represents an actual physical sequence of physical effects.

The boxes in Figure 10.2 stand for functions. No one wishes to imply that there is a bounded component or a specific locality in the brain that corresponds to the boxes. Quite the contrary. Those functions must occur at all levels of the hierarchy, even at the lowest levels acting at the tip of your tongue or in your little toe. But the theory nevertheless postulates that there must be components (clusters and connections of neurons) somewhere that carry out the functions named in the boxes. Powers (1973b) gives a little biological detail, but it will be many years before the map of the correspondence between functions and biological components does not have its larger part labeled "terra incognita." At present, the urgent task is to check the functioning of control systems as systems. About component and system, Powers says:

> The laws which govern the behavior of a complex system, therefore, are not the laws that govern the individual components of that system. The laws governing the individual components contain no statements about how those components shall be interconnected, nor do they impose any limits on possible interconnections (other than setting the number of *all possible* interconnections). Furthermore, there is no possible way to analyze a given system property into a *necessary* set of component properties, because any given system property could be brought about through assembling components in an immense variety of ways. Those way are equivalent at the system level, but not at the component level. (1980, p. 219)

Modeling

As I said earlier, the diagram is vastly oversimplified. In fact, Figure 10.2 is too simple to serve as a guide to actual experimentation with control theory. In the next chapter, you will come upon a somewhat more complicated diagram—Figure 11.6. It exemplifies a diagram that can serve as a guide to modeling. It illustrates how a more complex system must be made up of replications and hierarchies and more complex interconnections of basic units—a feature one would expect to see in a model that works the way a living creature works. In Chapter 11, I will explain how the diagram served as a guide to designing an experiment and constructing a working model of human behavior. Powers has provided a still more complicated diagram: see Powers (1979c, Part III, p. 107).

I have been using the word "model" here in a very special sense. I do not mean description, theory, procedure, ideal, or something to be emulated. I mean what Powers and Marken mean—an actual, tangible thing that will behave the same way the real thing behaves. So far, the "tangible things" have been programs in computers. I will say more about modeling in Chapter 11 under "The Model."

THE HIERARCHY

Humans are much more complicated than Figure 10.2 or 11.6. We are full of control systems of the sort shown in Figure 10.2, layers upon layers of them. We control perceptions having to do with eating, walking, talking, working, loving, getting information, fighting, and all the rest of our doings. There must be many connections among the individual systems in the circuitry of the neural net, and the connections can be neither haphazard nor of equal sway. Some control systems must set standards for others. An internal standard for wanting to perceive yourself having arrived at the library can require perceptions that your legs are carrying out the right motions for walking. But the internal standards for walking properly cannot very well require the perception that you are heading for the library; you wouldn't be able to walk to any other place. So there must be a hierarchy of control.

The higher levels of control must set standards for lower levels; the output quantities of the upper levels must be signals that alter standards lower in the hierarchy. (The outputs of the higher systems do not activate muscles; they become inputs to the internal standards of the lower-level systems that do.) The lower levels must, in return, keep the higher levels informed about perceptions coming in. The lower levels must not only send perceptions to their own comparators, but must also forward the perceptions upward, as in Figure 11.6 in the next chapter.

Powers postulates eleven levels of control system in the human. The list that follows differs somewhat from an earlier version (1973b); I took this from a sheet he handed out at the 1988 meeting of the Control System Group. The level numbered "1st" is the "lowest," and the "11th" the "highest."

Levels of Control Systems and Internal Standards

1st. *Intensity.*

2nd. Quality of *sensation.*

3rd. *Configuration*, position, perception of invariants.

The first three levels deliver static perceptions. The higher levels organize perceptions over time.

4th. *Transition*, change, tracking, control of movement and other changes of configuration, sensation, and intensity.

5th. *Event.*

6th. *Relationship.*

7th. *Category.*

8th. *Sequence*, routines, episodes.

9th. *Program*, rationality, language. Working your way to a goal along a path containing choices among sequences.

10th. *Principle*, strategy, heuristics. Values in the sense of what one puts consummatory goodness on. Going by intermittent evidence. Averaging instances.

11th. *System* conception, perceiving organized entities. Images of what the world is like.

Those are the levels of the hierarchy. I will not take space here to put more words on them one after another. I have already said some things about hierarchy in this and previous chapters, and I will say more as I go along; I'll trust that much to be sufficient. You will find an experiment on hierarchy recounted in Chapter 11 under "Hierarchy." If you want more, you can find all the levels except "event" and "category" described in successive chapters of Powers's (1973b) book.

I do not want the word "hierarchy" to put into your mind a diagram like the line organization of an army. A chart of a classical line organization is like a tree, in which no branch or twig grows over into another branch or twig. Every superior passes orders only to his or her subordinates and to nobody else's. The hierarchy of the neural circuitry is not like that. It is more like the rule in the army that any general can, upon occasion, command obedience from any colonel, any colonel from any major, and so on down, regardless of who is ordinarily in charge of a particular group of soldiers carrying out a particular task.

Here are some remarks by Powers (1980) about internal standards (purposes, goals) and the hierarchy:

> A purpose is not an intended *action*, but an intended *consequence* of action. Furthermore, in the final analysis, it is an intended state of an inner representation of that consequence—an intended state of perception.(p. 230)

> It is not as if a single spasmodic action had to produce a predestined future consequence. The control system is always right there, continually altering its actions to keep the sensed consequence what it is intended to be (one level of sensed consequence could be a steady approach toward some final relationship). (p. 231)

> Any action is at the same time an *intended goal*, continuously achieved, and a *variable means* adjusted according to the requirements of higher-order goals and external disturbances. The degree of volition one senses depends on whether he is focusing on the intended action (as the goal state of a perception of action) or on the higher-order *reason* for the action, the higher-order goal served by the action. When attention is on the higher-order goal, the lower-level action is sensed as *output*; when the attention is focused on the intentional nature of the lower-level action, the same action is sensed as an *input*, a perceived and controlled consequence of an output of still lower level (say, "effort"). (p. 234)

> What can be said about the higher levels is mostly negative. We *do not* know the basis on which the highest-level goals are set. We are *incapable* of tracing them to any specific external circumstances, particularly not present-time circumstances. We can offer some reasonable conjectures about how biochemical and genetic factors enter, particularly in connection with learning, but we can *by no acceptable scientific means* show that those factors are "ultimate" determinants, not in any sense. It is time to stop trying to make everything fit nineteenth-century ideas of physical determinism, which are based on little more than an allergic reaction to religion. The upper regions of human organization are a mystery which we have barely begun to approach; we will never understand them on the basis of a jab-and-jerk model of behavior. (p. 236)

Internal standards at one level can get into conflict with one another. That is, two control systems can make incompatible demands on control systems lower down. For example, I might hold to two principles, one of honesty and one of fair recompense. If I do not have an internal standard at the higher level of system concept to order those two principles, I can find myself with internal conflict. As long as I can get fair compensation for any labor in an honest way, I am all right. But if I go on for a long time getting paid less than I think my work is worth, what am I to do? I start to figure out a way to cheat the company out of some money. But then my principle of honesty makes my conscience hurt, and I look again for some honest way to get my salary increased. But I cannot think of a way that would get me enough money. So I start thinking again about some skulduggery. Back and forth I oscillate, using up attention and energy that could be put to better use. If I am lucky, I reorganize my hierarchy. I might move honesty up to the level of system concept. That is, I might come to view the social world as unworkable unless people (including me) are honest. I would believe not just that honesty is a good thing, but that I would be throwing sand into the gears of the world in which I live if I am dishonest. Or I might move honesty down to the level of program and add it, in my mind, to the company's rules. That is, I would consider honesty to be any act that does not flagrantly break a clear rule. Or I might think of some other way to rearrange things to keep conflict from occurring.

But if there is such a multiplicity of possible standards in individual humans, where is there a possibility for a science? First, let us give up hopeless quests. Hunting for a few ruling components, such as a catalog of personality traits, clearly has not worked. So it is the better part of valor to give up and hunt for some way of going about it that does work. Second, let us look for the invariants—for the internal procedures or processes that always work in the same way. So far, small though the body of experimentation may be, it is clear that one invariant is the maintenance of match between the incoming perception and the internal standard.

Here is an analogy with the study of evolution. How is it that we can consider the study of evolution to be scientific, when evolution produces millions of different species? Students of evolution use the strategy of looking for the invariant processes by which those millions of forms of bodies and brains serve some purpose for their occupants—they look for some ruling principle, procedure, or process in all that variety. They infer that the bodies and brains in various environments make it possible for the creatures to maintain their inputs through using their environmental niches in their specific ways. When there are more of certain kinds of opportunities and difficulties in certain environments, the adaptation enables the collective creature (its population) or perhaps its genes to maintain the necessary perceptual inputs to its individuals.

REORGANIZATION

One more feature of Powers's theory is too important to be omitted even from this brief account. Overall or throughout the eleven levels, says Powers (1973b), there is another function that ties them all together and enables adaptations at one level to bring about changes at several or all other levels. Although the higher levels do shape our perceptions at lower levels over long periods of time, they do not do so unalterably or permanently. If they did, we could not learn much from experience. So there is a function that enables us to reorganize our internal standards up and down the levels. It keeps the whole organism in good working order. It moves things around to minimize internal conflicts. It recognizes threats, physical and otherwise, that demand first priority. You might call it self-preservation. If you prefer the current lingo, you might call it survival. Powers calls this function *reorganization*. It is a special kind of learning.

In ordinary discourse, we use the word "learning" in two different ways. One is to mean memorizing; we say that we "learn" someone's name. Or suppose we find our way for the first time to the boss's office. When we have made the correct left and right turns and have used the correct up or down elevator, we say we have "learned" the way to the boss's office. You could as easily say that we have found it and memorized it. I realize that some people will say I am vastly simplifying matters—that there are certainly more than two kinds of learning. I do not want to quarrel. I think that reorganization is different from any other kind. It is all right with me if other people want to classify those other kinds into subcategories.

Reorganization, the second kind of learning, revises what is worth memorizing, which goals are worth pursuing, which programs are worth building— which internal standards, in short, are worth matching by controlling perceptual input. Reorganization is the kind of learning that shows us new meanings: new relationships between ourselves and others, new programs for organizing our routines, and new boundaries and new vistas concerning the systems within which we conceive ourselves to be working. It is the kind of learning through which we transcend the mechanical and routine effects of experience. It does not necessarily require conscious thought. It can occur quietly, while we are not looking, so to speak, or it can occur like the blast of trumpets or the singing of angels—as insight and aha! This kind of learning often makes us feel regenerated, enlarged, inspired, in command of new powers.

This kind of learning is not something to be taught. It is not a lesson to be learned at nine o'clock on Thursday morning. It comes to you—to you alone— at that terrible and wonderful and magical moment when you find that your categories, your programs, your principles have been playing you false and will no longer serve. You then pull yourself up by your bootstraps and find in yourself a newness—a newness that you did not plan and that no one could plan for you, a newness that your marvelous brain made for you while you were not even expecting it to happen.

There you have it: eleven hierarchical levels for controlling perceptions (input) and one function (reorganization) to keep everything in trim. When you consider the great variety of environmental events (disturbances) we encounter, all the kinds of dangers we avoid, and all the dangers we do not quite avoid but somehow manage to surmount in myriad and ingenious ways, it is not surprising that we have developed, over the millions of years, such a phantasmagorically complex but marvelously capable neural net.

SUMMARY OF POSTULATES

I will now recapitulate very briefly what I think are the core features of Powers's control theory, though I risk oversimplification. The theory:

—assumes that humans are a natural kind, a species, with invariants within and among individuals.

—takes control of perception as a fact to be explained.

—postulates a complete, circular feedback loop. At the lowest levels of the hierarchy, some parts of the loop lie in the neural net and some in the environment. All parts within the neural net act at once.

—postulates that the feedback loop contains the functions shown in Figure 10.2: perceptual input, internal standard, comparator, internal processing to produce an output quantity, and others. In the loops at the bottom of the hierarchy, the output quantity, through the feedback function, opposes the disturbance function arising in the environment. Higher in the hierarchy, the output quantities reset the internal standards of loops at lower levels.

—postulates a hierarchy of levels of control. Outputs of loops higher in the hierarchy always control the internal standards of loops lower down, never the reverse.

—postulates that the neural net now and again reorganizes itself to minimize overall "intrinsic" errors. It alters assortments and weightings of loops in many regions of the net, altering, in effect, the "content" or "meaning" of higher-level standards such as principles and system-concepts.

—provides a guide to modeling by enabling the experimenter to predict an input quantity the person will hold constant and therefore that the model must also hold constant. Experiments can then be quantitative not in the sense of statistics about a population, but in the sense of accurate prediction of the consequences of the acts (not the acts themselves) of each individual.

THE TEST

By now, you have probably been wondering about study design. Designs for survey research, designs that correlate inputs and outputs, and experimental designs using control groups—the designs I discussed in Chapters 2 through 7—surely cannot be used in the method of specimens. You have probably also been thinking that study design in the method of specimens must have a lot to do with finding internal standards. That is right. Sometimes, using the method of specimens, you can ask people to adopt a particular standard temporarily. I gave examples of that in this chapter under "The Rubber Bands." You will of course design your experiment so that you can check constantly on whether the person is indeed maintaining the standard you asked the person to maintain. At other times, you will not be able to ask the person to adopt a standard from you. Even if the person is willing, the person may not understand your request sufficiently well. Then you must hunt for the internal standard.

Powers had described a procedure for finding an internal standard. He calls the procedure simply The Test (for which see Powers, 1973b, pp. 232-46; and 1979c, Part IV, pp. 110, 112).

The Test goes like this (adapted from Powers, 1979c, Part IV, p. 112):

1. Select a variable you think the person might be maintaining at some level. In other words, guess at an input quantity.

2. Predict what will happen if the person is *not* maintaining the variable at a preferred level.

3. Apply various amounts and directions of disturbance directly to the variable.

4. Measure the actual effects of the disturbances.

5. If the effects are what you predicted under the assumption that the person is *not* acting to control the variable, stop here. The person is indeed not acting to control it; you guessed wrong about the variable.

6. If an actual effect is markedly smaller than the predicted effect, look for what the person might be doing to oppose the disturbance. Look for a cause of the opposition to the disturbance which, by its own varying, can counterbalance variations in the input quantity. That cause may be caused by the person's output. You may have found the feedback function.

7. Look for the way the person can sense the variable. If you can find no way the person could sense the variable, the input quantity, stop. People cannot control what they cannot sense.

8. If you find a means of sensing, block it so that the person cannot now sense the variable. If the disturbance continues to be opposed, you have not found the right sensor. If you cannot find a sensor, stop. Make another guess at an input quantity.

9. If all of the above steps are passed, you have found the input quantity, the variable the person is controlling.

Using The Test is not easy. You must make guesses about internal standards and then change something in the environment that the person senses. If you succeed in changing it—if the person does *not* act to maintain it the way it was—then you have guessed wrong; there is nothing about the change you made that disturbed an input the person wants to maintain. If the person *does* act against the change you try to make, then you have guessed right, or at least you are on the right track. You know something more about the person than you did before. Of course, you may have guessed wrong about the feature of the change, the input quantity, you think the person is rectifying. You will find that out when your later predictions go wrong. Then you have to guess again, though you are ahead of the game, because you know the input has something to do with the change you tried to make in the environment. So after you guess right about one kind of environmental change the person will oppose, even though you missed the input quantity embedded in it, your second guess has a much better chance of being close to the mark than your first guess had. Still, you never know when the person might reorganize the internal standards. If that happens, then you must start over.

Predicting the direction of behavior people will exhibit—or in practical life, to predict the direction of behavior of a person you care about—requires being able to anticipate with some accuracy the internal standards the person will bring into play. The Test is a systematic guide to ferreting out internal standards. To learn the perceptual inputs an individual is maintaining, The Test, though sometimes lengthy, promises shorter searches and fewer wild-goose chases than the methods currently most in use by social scientists.

If you want to read more about control theory, the following are some writings that can be dug up without too much effort: Baum, Reese, and Powers (1973), Bohannan, Powers, and Schoepfle (1974), Hershberger (1989), Marken (1980, 1982, 1983, 1985, 1986, 1988). Mary Powers (1987), W. T. Powers (1971, 1973a, 1973b, 1975, 1976, 1977, 1978, 1979a, 1979b, 1979c, 1980, 1987, 1989), Powers, Clark and McFarland (1960), van de Rijt-Plooij (1986), and W. D. Williams (1986). There is also a large body of research lying mostly in the field known as "human factors" that exemplifies the strong predictability that can be achieved with the concept of the feedback loop. An especially large program of work in that field has been reviewed by T. J. Smith and K. U. Smith (1988).

11

Testing Specimens

Here I will tell about four experiments using the method of specimens and designed as investigations of control theory. The first three test for visual invariants at the lower levels of the hierarchy. The last tests a hypothesis about an invariant at one of the highest levels—the maintenance of a self-concept.

WHAT IS THE PERSON DOING?

Whatever people are doing, they are pursuing purposes and controlling perceptions to do so. Within control theory, indeed, "pursuing purposes" and "controlling perceptions" are almost synonymous. But researchers who do not habitually look for control of perceptions in behavior often have difficulty in believing it even when they see it. All experiments designed according to control theory exhibit the fact of control, but Powers devised a demonstration that is especially dramatic in showing that people control the perceptual consequences of their acts. People initiate acts and guide the progress of their actions, but only to control the perceptual consequences that result. As I write, Powers has not yet published an account of this demonstration, though he described it at the meeting of the American Society for Cybernetics in St. Gallen, Switzerland, in March of 1987.

Procedure

The subject sits before a computer screen with joystick in hand. Perhaps you have not operated a joystick. It is a small lever poised vertically and moored at the bottom by a ball joint. The top end can be rotated in any direction. Think of the gearshift on the floor of an automobile and then imagine it to be only three or four inches in height.

When the joystick is moved this way and that, a dot on the right-hand side of the screen mirrors the motion. The computer is programmed so that the connection between the top end of the joystick and the position of the dot on the screen is direct and linear. One unit of angular motion of the joystick produces one unit of movement of the dot on the screen and in a corresponding direction.

The screen also shows a dot at the left side. When the joystick moves circularly, as if its top end were describing a circle, the left-hand dot follows the motion directly, just as the right-hand dot does. But when the joystick moves radially, either inward toward the circle's center or outward away from the center, something else happens. Actually, a "home" circle is specified by the program in the computer. The speed of radial movement of the left-hand dot changes according to where the joystick (and of course the right-hand dot, too) lies in relation to the home circle. For radial motion, the link between the motion of the joystick and the left-hand dot is not linear, but accelerated. When the joystick (or the right-hand dot) lies on the home circle, the left-hand dot does not move radially. But when the joystick lies away from the circle (either inside or outside), the distance of the joystick or right-hand dot from the home circle specifies the *rate* of radial motion of the left-hand dot. The farther the joystick lies from the home circle, the faster the left-hand dot will move radially.

The right-hand dot provides a direct record of the movements of the joystick. But the relation between the joystick and what the left-hand dot is doing, the relation itself, shifts as the position of the joystick changes either toward or away from the home circle.

The subject is asked to draw a figure with the *left-hand* dot. The experimenter does not tell the subject the nature of the connections between the joystick and the dots. The experimenter tells the subject only to draw whatever figure the subject wishes with the left-hand dot. The subject must then move the joystick in whatever manner necessary to produce the figure the subject has chosen.

Results

Figure 11.1 shows what one subject did. On the left, we see that the subject chose to draw two squares and a triangle. On the right, we see the direct record of the movements the subject made with the joystick to produce the figures at the left. The experiment demonstrates dramatically the fact that the subject was controlling his perceptions of what the left-hand dot was doing. He moved the joystick in whatever way necessary to enable himself to perceive that the dot was describing the figures he wanted to see it describe. If you were watching

Figure 11.1
Act and Purpose

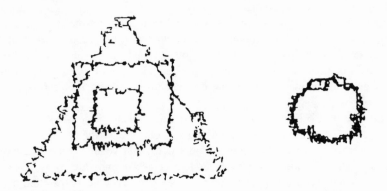

Source: William T. Powers, interview with Laurence Richards, 1987. Used by permission.

only the subject's hand or only the right-hand part of the screen, you would not have a clue to what the subject was doing.

If, for example, a supervisor had told a worker to draw a square, we would not be surprised if, watching only the right-hand trace, the supervisor were soon to say, "Hey, I thought I told you to draw a square!" Here, however, as in a good many ordinary situations we see no clue to the person's intention in the detailed acts of his hand. In every case, no matter what figure the subject chooses to draw, we see the subject's hand moving, with some seeming inaccuracies, around a circle. Except in those cases where the subject actually does choose to draw a circle, we would always guess wrong about what the subject is doing.

And we would be wrong, too, about the "inaccuracies." The small deviations from the circle at the right side of the screen look like error, but they are not. They are in fact the small, necessary, purposeful movements by which the subject moves the left-hand dot in the pattern he wants to see. The right-hand side of the screen shows the person's *act*, but the left side shows what the person was *doing*.

Assumptions

The first thing taken for granted here, of course, is the fact of control of perception. If the person could not see (perceive) the left side of the screen, the person could have no way of knowing how much or in what direction the dot was moving; he could draw a figure only in imagination. If the subject were blindfolded, given a pencil, and asked to draw a square on paper, he could do a fair job of it because of the direct connection between the sensed hand-motion and the line on the paper. But with the complicated connection

Powers built between the hand of the subject and the cursor movement, no vividness of imagination would be sufficient for success.

The experiment assumes that all humans act this way. Can you imagine, once the person accepts the task, that any physically normal person would perform differently? You do not need to count proportions of people who behave as predicted or test for statistical significance. You do not need to run a "control group"—what meaning could that idea have here?

No assumptions about language are needed. The experimenter does not need to wonder whether the subject understands the instructions. Once the subject produces a figure with the left-hand dot, it does not matter whether the subject actually heard the experimenter talking or just happened to feel an urge at that moment to draw a figure.

An important assumption is that we can learn how behavior is managed only if we track it on the same time scale that it actually occurs. Suppose someone had given the instruction, had then walked out of the room, had kept no record of the subject's hand movements, and had come back later to find a square showing on the screen. That observer would naturally suppose that the subject's hand had moved in a square to produce the square on the screen, and it would be easy to conclude that the instruction had set in motion a square-drawing routine for the hand to carry out. That conclusion would result from taking observations at times far more widely spaced than required to reveal the pattern at the right side of Figure 11.1. The moment-to-moment record made by the computer tells a very different story.

What Is Remarkable?

That demonstration shows with remarkable clarity the fact that living creatures control their perceptions; it also shows their skill in doing so. Furthermore, the experiment shows the hierarchy in the neural net. The internal standard for the intended figure is necessary to set the standards for directions and amounts of hand movement, but the reverse is not true. Our ability to move our hands in various directions and amounts does not tell us what figures to draw.

The demonstration shows plainly how we can be deceived by appearances: (1) how we can go wrong by focusing on acts (the right side of the screen) instead of purposes (the left side) and (2) how we can go wrong if we take the line through the middle of the dots (in this case the home circle amid the dots at the right) as the real thing and call the deviations from it "error." I made this second point in Chapter 5 about regression lines.

INTENTION

Many psychologists want to study purposes and intentions but the *S-O-R* conception makes it difficult. All behavior is a means to an end. Sometimes the

Figure 11.2
Video Display

|

|

eventual purpose for an immediate behavior is difficult to divine. But the immediate intentions are often very clear: hitting a golf ball, writing a letter,
driving to the grocery store. Marken (1982) set up an experiment to show how
intention can be discerned quantitatively in the laboratory without having to
rely on the subject's verbal report.

Procedure

The subject sat at a video monitor displaying two vertical lines, as in Figure
11.2. The subject was asked to choose one of the lines, the upper or the lower,
and move it back and forth across the screen by pressing the left and right
arrow-keys. The lines did not move, however, in linear relation to key presses.
The computer was programmed to insert slow random disturbances between the
key and the lines. Furthermore, pressing either key added movement to *both*
lines, though at different rates. Pressing the left-arrow key, for example, added
leftward movement to *both* lines, but at randomly different rates.

It was impossible to tell the line the subject had chosen by watching the
screen or examining recorded plots of points. The subject was not told to maintain any regular pattern, but was free to change direction and speed at will.
Nevertheless, if the subject was following directions, the movement of one line
was by intent, and the movement of the other was an irrelevant side-effect.

The crux of the experiment is the fact that the subject must, indeed, act to
control a perception and therefore act against disturbances. If the subject were
to do nothing—to touch neither arrow-key—then of course the chosen line would
follow exactly the random movements programmed for it. The correlation over
moments in time between the programmed disturbance and the position of the
line on the screen would then be 1.0, since there would be no other effect on
the line. But as soon as the subject acts to move one of the lines, then that line
will move according to the sum of the effects of the randomization and the key
presses. And to make the line go where the subject wants it to go, the subject
must of course counteract the effects of the random disturbance. Since random
points must deviate randomly from almost any regular pattern of points, the
subject's counteractions to produce a regular pattern of movement of the line
will produce positions of the line on the screen that have a correlation close to
zero with the randomly programmed positions.

Marken's prediction was that the subject would succeed very well in controlling the movement of the chosen line despite the random disturbance, with

Table 11.1
Correlations between Disturbances and Positions of Upper and Lower Lines*

Trial	Subject RM Intended line	Subject RM Other line	Subject LH Intended line	Subject LH Other line
1	.06 L	.40	.12 U	.22
2	-.04 U	.31	-.03 L	.43
3	-.13 L	.37	-.16 L	.57
4	-.02 U	.28	.06 L	.14
5	-.04 U	.40	.09 U	.26
6	-.09 U	.31	.25 L	.40
7	-.07 L	.34	.25 U	.28
8	-.02 L	.32	.03 L	.38
9	-.04 U	.46	.23 U	.36
10	-.11 L	.41	.06 U	.34
Means	-.05	.36	.09	.34
Range	-.13 to +.06	+.28 to +.46	-.16 to +.25	+.14 to +.57

*"U" and "L" tell whether the subject reported intending to move the upper or lower line.

Source: Adapted from Marken (1982, Table 1, p. 649).

the result that the correlation between the positions of the line and the random disturbance would be very much less than 1.0. But the key-pressing by the subject would have much less effect on the other line, since the subject would let it go wherever it went without trying to prevent it. Marken predicted that the correlation between the random disturbance and the other line would always be higher than that between the disturbance and the chosen line.

Results

Marken ran two subjects, each in ten trials of one minute each. The correlations between line positions and disturbances are shown in Table 11.1.

Before each trial, subjects wrote down the line they intended to move. The lines are indicated in the table by "U" for the upper line and "L" for the lower. Actually, that information is almost superfluous, since the results showed that, for both subjects on every trial, their intentions were unambiguously differentiated by the correlations. As Marken predicted, the average of the differences in correlation was large, though two of those for subject LH were small—a difference of only .08 in trial 4 and of .03 in trial 7. The largest differences were those of .50 for RM at trials 3 and 9 and .73 for LH at trial 3.

Why was the correlation with the other line always higher than that with the intended line? There was nothing in the set-up that would have brought the correlation between the positions of one of the lines and the random disturbances close to zero except the control—the opposition to the disturbances—being exerted by the subject. The two correlations would have been higher and more alike in value, for example, if the subject had merely pressed the keys lackadaisically, from occasional urges to relieve the boredom of sitting in one place.

The more unremitting the subject's insistence on opposing the random disturbance to the chosen line, the closer to zero the correlation would go. The impressive feature of the outcome is not the fact that one or the other correlation was always lower—that is inevitable if only by the nature of arithmetic. The impressive feature is that one of the correlations was so often very close to zero. Then, when we get the information that the lesser correlation was always attached to the line the subject intended to control, the outcome is still more impressive.

What else might have happened but did not? If the subject had tried to press the keys randomly, the resulting correlations would have been much closer to each other than those in Table 11.1. When a correlation had been calculated over moments in time, for each line, between the randomly programmed disturbance and the position of the line, the difference between the correlation for the chosen line and that for the unchosen line would have been much less than the differences in Table 11.1. If the subject were to press the keys at a uniform rate regardless of the movement the subject would see the line making, the correlation would be 1.0, since the addition of a constant amount to the randomly programmed points would produce an exactly parallel series of points. But if the subject presses the keys so as to produce an intended motion of a chosen line by *counteracting* the effect of the random disturbance, then we will get the kind of pattern we see in Marken's results.

Assumptions

Marken's experiment assumes circular causation in a feedback loop; the subject acts at every moment to maintain the desired movement of the line despite disturbances from the computer that would otherwise disrupt the motion.

You do not need to run a control group; you do not need to assume that people in a first group are behaving the way the people in a second group would behave if they were in the first group. You do not have to assume substitutability of persons within the experiment. You must, however, make the assumption of species; that is, that every normal member of the species functions by the same principles. In this case, the assumption is that every normal member of the species can exert control in a way that brings the correlation between the line position and the random disturbances close to zero.

You do not have to count a proportion of people to know whether the experiment has succeeded, nor do you have to calculate a correlation over people. Tests of statistical significance are not needed.

The use of words in this experiment was reduced to the few words used by the experimenter to give instructions. The experimenter did not, however, have to rest on hope that his words were understood. That could be told from the data in the case of every subject. The experimenter needed no more than one of two words from the subjects—either "upper" or "lower." And once a few experiments on intention have been run, you do not need language to get evidence of the intention.

You do not have to define a "right answer" in advance. You do not have to specify a pattern of motion you will accept as proper evidence. You can accept any motion the subject chooses to produce.

You do not look for a high correlation between stimulus and response. You look for a near-zero correlation between environmental events and a perceptual input which, if not controlled, would vary along with the environmental events. In this case, the environmental event was the random disturbance to the lines on the screen, and the input was the subject's perception of the chosen line moving in the desired way.

What Is Remarkable?

The experimenter instructed the subject to choose a line and move it back and forth across the screen. The subject did that. What is remarkable about that? The point of this experiment, of course, was not that the experimenter succeeded in getting the subject to follow instructions, but rather (1) to show that humans behave as if they have purposes or intentions, (2) to show that you can discover an intention even in a situation where the naked eye cannot discern the part of the environment the person is acting upon, and (3) you can make that discovery if you know about control theory. The experiment also shows clearly, once again, that a human can adopt an internal standard from another human and then maintain a perception that agrees closely with that standard by simple actions (key presses) despite the completely random motion of the feature of the environment that must be acted against.

The experiment seems simple. It will seem less so if you read the original report. It will seem even less so if you try to design a similar experiment yourself. And it will seem still less so if you think for a moment about all the argument in the psychological literature about purposes and intentions and other inner states.

Figure 11.3
Video Display

|

|

|

HIERARCHY

An essential postulate of control theory is the hierarchical organization of the feedback loops in the neural net. Marken (1986) carried out a series of three experiments to show how hierarchical control can operate in apparently simple behavior and to show, too, how hierarchical control can be modeled. I will recount here the first experiment of the three.

Procedure

The subject sat before a computer screen that displayed three vertical lines arranged as in Figure 11.3. The two outer lines were black, the middle one blue. Also in front of the subject were two paddle-handles. The handles could be rotated. The subject was asked to turn the handles as necessary to keep the width between the left-hand line and the middle line as close as possible to the width between the middle line and the right-hand line, and to keep both of those widths as close to two centimeters as reasonably convenient. That was the only instruction given.

The subject held a handle in each hand. The computer was programmed so that the left-hand handle affected the left-hand line, and the right-hand handle affected the middle line. Neither handle affected the right-hand line. In addition, the positions of the lines were varied by three slowly varying random disturbances, all different, one applied to each line. The three lines, therefore, moved continuously and unpredictably back and forth on the screen, and the subject's task, in effect, was to add movement to the left and middle lines in such a way as to keep the distances from the middle line to the outer lines equal, no matter what the right-hand line did. At all times, the positions of the three lines were all that were visible to the subject. Each subject was tested in several two-minute sessions. The random disturbances were changed from session to session. Six adults served as subjects.

Results

The results for one subject for the last 90 seconds of one run are shown in Figure 11.4. Part (a) of the figure shows the traces of the three lines. Q1 labels

Figure 11.4
Position and Distance Traces For One Subject

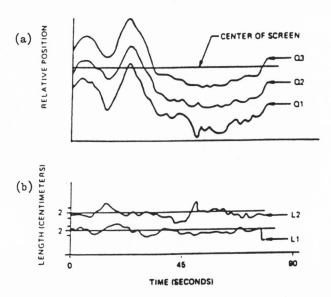

Source: Adapted from Marken (1986, Figure 3, p. 272).

the trace of the left-hand line, Q2 the middle line, and Q3 the right-hand line. You can see that the two outer traces keep very much the same distance from the middle one. Part (b) shows in another way the subject's success in maintaining the two distances equal. There, L1 labels the curve representing the distance from the left-hand line to the middle one, and L2 labels the distance from the middle line to the right-hand one.

The subject's purpose, the perception the subject undertook to maintain, might seem a simple one—to keep three little lines equally spaced. It is no more complicated, surely, than keeping an automobile in its lane while driving along a curving road. But the experiment illustrates beautifully how much delicately coordinated bodily movement a living creature brings to the simplest act. Part (a) of Figure 11.5 shows the traces of the three random disturbances (D1, D2, D3) against which the subject (the same subject as in Figure 11.4) had to act. Part (b) of the figure shows how the subject's two hands (H1, H2) moved. It is clear from Figure 11.5 that the two hands had to act independently to maintain the equal distances. Indeed, the correlation between the two handle-traces averaged over subjects was only .25.

Note that the subject could control only the *positions* of the left and middle lines. That is, one hand controlled one line and the other another, independently. But giving the two hands control of two lines did not guarantee equal distances. The two hands could produce an infinity of positions of the two lines

Figure 11.5
Disturbance Traces (D1, D2, and D3) and Handle-Position Traces (H1 and H2)
For One Subject

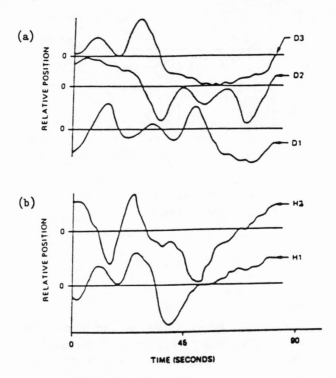

Source: Adapted from Marken (1986, Figure 3, p. 272).

without producing equal distances. Marken reasoned that not only control of the positions of the two lines, but also another feature of control, had to exist to select only those positions that would give equal distances. The lowest level of control would receive perceptions of the positions of the three lines. Then there had to be a higher level of control that would compare those perceptions and check whether the two distances were equal. That higher level of control would alter the internal standards of the lower level (alter, that is, the subject's notion of where a line "ought" to be) so as to maintain the two distances equal and near to two centimeters.

One way Marken demonstrated the existence of hierarchical control was through the use of a measure he calls the "stability factor." Let V_e be the expected variance of a controlled variable (such as the position of a line or the distance between two of them) and let V_o be the observed variance. For example, the expected variance of the distance from the left line to the middle one is equal to the sum of the variances of (1) the random disturbance applied to the left

Table 11.2
Stability Indexes

	Variable			
	L_1	L_2	Q_1	Q_2
	Subject 1			
Run 1	-10.2	-9.2	-1.1	-1.3
Run 2	-12.2	-13.8	-1.1	-1.2
	Subject 2			
Run 1	-7.6	-8.9	-0.88	-0.72
Run 2	-9.8	-10.3	-0.99	-0.87
	Averages for six subjects			
Means	-11.0	-10.7	-1.0	-1.1

Source: Excerpted from Marken (1986, Table 1, p. 273).

line, (2) the random disturbance applied to the middle line, (3) the positions of the handle affecting the left line, and (4) the positions of the handle affecting the middle line. The observed variance of that distance is simply the variance of the distance between the two lines on the screen over the course of an experimental run. Other variances can be arrived at similarly. The formula for the stability index is:

$$S = 1 - (V_e/V_o)^{\frac{1}{2}}$$

If the observed variance is fully as great as the expected variance, then S is zero, which means that the subject is effecting no control. If S is less than one (that is, negative), then the subject is reducing the observed variance and counteracting disturbances. The index S is in units of standard deviations away from the condition of no control; the larger the negative value of S, the more precise will be the control.

Table 11.2 shows the stability indexes for two experimental runs of each of two individual subjects, and also the averages for all six subjects. In the table, L_1 stands for the distance from the left-hand line to the middle one, L_2 the distance from the middle line to the right-hand one, Q_1 the position of the left-hand line, and Q_2 the position of the middle line.

The *distances* L_1 and L_2 are controlled variables, just as are the *positions* Q_1 and Q_2. We see in the table that the average stability indexes for L_1 and L_2

were -11.0 and -10.7, in both cases more than 10 standard deviations away from a completely uncontrolled condition. Though a predicted result more than 10 standard deviations away from a null hypothesis is as rare as hen's teeth in social science, that fact is of small moment here. The usefulness of the stability index here is in comparing the amounts of control at the two levels of the hierarchy. The averages of the stability indexes for Q_1 and Q_2 are both about -1.0. That figure indicates a good deal of control (a ratio of V_e to V_o of four to one), but much less than that at the higher level. This result fits the prediction; the higher internal standard, distance, sets the lower standard, position. Therefore the standards for position were varied somewhat over time by the higher standard, and the observed variance of the positions Q_1 and Q_2 was therefore greater than that of the distances L_1 and L_2.

One thing we have seen so far is that the subjects did, every one, succeed in keeping the two distances very closely the same. That seems hardly strange, because we are accustomed to witnessing such marvelous capabilities in humans. But we have also seen that the control over the perception of *distances* (which was the task the subjects accepted) was greater for every subject than the control over the perception of *positions*—just as the theory predicted.

The Model

Marken also built a model of this behavior in the form of a computer program. Since social scientists use the word "model" in many ways, I will explain what Marken and Powers mean by it. They mean an actual, tangible thing that will behave the same way the real thing behaves. In a model railroad, for example, trains run on tracks, forward and backward, they start and stop, and travel at various speeds. Cars couple and uncouple. They do those things just as real trains do. Of course, a model will not have the parts (components) that the real thing has, even scaled down. In most model railroads, in all the small ones, the "steam engines" look like real steam engines on the outside, but inside they have electric motors, not boilers and pipes. Nevertheless, the model engine succeeds in behaving in relation to its tracks (its environment) in exactly the same way a real engine behaves in relation to its tracks. You can use a model railroad to work out problems in complicated switching yards, and the solutions will work in the full scale. That is what I mean here (following Powers and Marken) by "model." I do not intend other meanings social scientists often give the word such as theory, description, procedure, or ideal. A model embodies theory; it is a realization of theory. The model (as the word is used here) is built from the specifications given by theory, and it is a tangible, physical thing that shows the same necessary internal functions that the thing modeled does.

In studying living creatures, we often do not know what their internal structures are like, and we certainly do not have the technology to build a replica with living tissues. We can, however, build a model with other materials and, if the model behaves the same way living creatures do, we can reason that whatever they are made of inside, and however their components are arranged, the *functions* in the model and their interrelations are mimicking some functions inside the living creature.

Marken's model in his computer was not part of the programming that enabled the subjects to affect the positions of the lines on the computer screen. That programming merely connected the handle movement to the line movement and added the random disturbance. Programming the computer to perform as a model and testing the model with humans were entirely separate operations.

I turn now to the equations that specify what the model must do. As before, L_1 and L_2 stand for the two distances, though now I am using the more conventional subscript notation. Similarly, Q_1, Q_2 and Q_3 stand for the positions of the three lines on the screen. Further, D_1, D_2, and D_3 will stand for the three random disturbances of line position, and H_1 and H_2 will stand for the effects on line position of the two handles operated by the subject.

Like the subjects, the model is required to keep the two distances the same, or equal to a constant value c, which in this case is two centimeters:

$$L_1 = L_2 = c \tag{1}$$

Since the positions of the first two lines are determined by the sum of the random disturbance and the handle position, while the position of the third line is determined only by the random disturbance applied to it, we have the following three specifications for dependencies within the model. Here (t) indicates temporal variations.

$$Q_{1(t)} = D_{1(t)} + H_{1(t)}$$

$$Q_{2(t)} = D_{2(t)} + H_{2(t)} \tag{2}$$

$$Q_{3(t)} = D_{3(t)}$$

The distances, of course, must be connected to the line positions as follows:

$$L_{1(t)} = Q_{2(t)} - Q_{1(t)}$$

$$\tag{3}$$

$$L_{2(t)} = Q_{3(t)} - Q_{2(t)}$$

Substituting appropriately from equations (1) and (2) into (3), we get these two equations for the ways the two handle positions will counteract the effects of the random disturbances in the model:

$$H_{1(t)} = D_{3(t)} - D_{1)t)} - 2c$$

(4)

$$H_{2(t)} = D_{3(t)} - D_{2(t)} - c$$

In effect, the task of the human subjects was to solve simultaneously the equations (4). That ability must now be added to the model. To show how Marken did that, I turn to Figure 11.6.

Figure 11.6 is a diagram of the model. It is not a "path diagram." The lines and arrows stand for actual electrical signals, and the boxes, ovals, and circles from and to which the arrows point stand for actual functions. Nobody claims that those functions are carried out in the computer by components that are built like living tissue, but only, if the model is to mirror human behavior, that the same functions must be carried out both in the computer and in the human, just as something must turn axles both in a real railroad engine and in its model.

To examine the figure, let us begin at the lower left corner. The loop we see there corresponds to Figure 10.2 in Chapter 10. In the environment, we see Q1 a physical quantity providing input to the neural net—or in the case of the model, a quantity that will be treated as input in the subsequent calculations the computer is programmed by the model to perform. Q1 is determined partly by the random disturbance $D1$, which the model-builder includes in the programming to simulate unpredictable events in the environment. Q1 is also partly determined by the handle position $H1$, which will be simulated by the output signal from this level-1 control system.

The little box labeled S (1,1) stands for the sensor at level 1 sending on the signal to system 1. The oval containing the summation sign, sigma, is there only for completeness; it will make more sense when I talk about it at level 2. P (1,1) stands for the perceptual signal coming in at level 1 in system 1. Note that it goes not only to the comparator in system 1, but also on up to the summation function at level 2. The comparator C compares the perception P (1,1) with the reference signal (internal standard) R (1,1) and sends out an error signal E (1,1). The effector function f (G_1, K_1) converts the error signal into instructions for action. In the human, the effector function would send signals to the muscles at H1. In the model, since there are no muscles, it simply sends the compensatory signal on to $Q1$. O (1,1) stands for the output signal to H1.

Moving to the right, we find system 2, which is built just like system 1. Farther to the right, we find system 3, but system 3 contains only input functions and signals, no outputs, because in the small universe of this experiment, our human and our model can perceive $Q3$ but cannot act upon it.

Now let us go to the top of the diagram, at level 2. The reference signals (internal standards) for distances, R (2,1) and R (2,2), are equal constants (two centimeters) put into the program by the model-builder. This is the specification given by equation (1). The input "perception" comes into system 2,1 (the

Figure 11.6
A Two-Level Hierarchy of Control

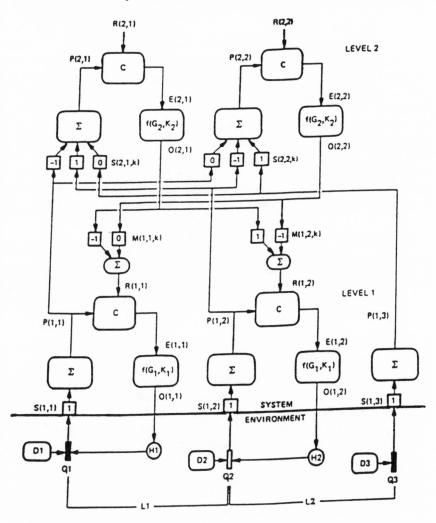

Source: Marken (1986, p. 270).

upper left-hand system) from the three systems at level 1. The signals from below are weighted at the boxes labeled S (2,1,k) and summed by the summation function indicated by the sigma. The input from system 1,1 is weighted at −1, and that from system 1,2 at +1. Their summation, then, subtracts the position of $Q1$ from the position of $Q2$, yielding the distance between them. The perceptual signal from system 1,3 is weighted at zero, and has no effect on the upper-level perceptual signal P (2,1).

The output O (2,1) from the upper-level system 2,1 goes downward to modify the reference signals of the level-1 systems. At the lower-level system 1,1, the output signal from upper-level system 2,1 is weighted at -1, and the output from system 2,2 is weighted at zero. The output from the upper-level system controlling the distance from $Q1$ to $Q2$ sets the reference signal R (1,1) to tell the lower-level comparator how much $Q1$ should be moved to stay at the right distance from $Q2$. The output from the upper-level system 2,2 has no effect (weighted zero), because $Q1$ will be most accurately placed if its position depends only on $Q2$.

You can trace out the other connections similarly. There are some technicalities connected with the effector functions that are needed to make the computer simulate a continuously acting feedback loop, but I will omit them from this description. The information put into the programming of the model by the model-builder to simulate the conditions under which the human subject worked enables the model to solve equations (4) from moment to moment. The information includes the reference values R (i,j), the weights S (i,j,k) and M (i,j,k), and the effector functions f (G_i, K_i).

I might note that in a more complex "creature," other systems at level 1 would be complete loops, not truncated like system 1,3 in the diagram, and the perceptual inputs at level 2 would not stop there, but would have branches going on up to higher-level systems, just as the perceptions from level 1 in the diagram branch off to go up to level 2.

The Fit of the Model

How well did Marken's computer model succeed in behaving like his human subjects? To test the fit, Marken calculated the correlations between the positions of the line $Q1$ produced by the model and those produced by the subject when both model and subject were working against the same three disturbances. In the same way, he calculated correlations for $Q2$ and the handle-positions $H1$ and $H2$. He could not calculate useful correlations for $L1$ and $L2$, because the variances in those values produced by the model were too small—almost zero. Table 11.3 shows the correlations for the other four variables, each calculated from 400 data-pairs. The table shows data for two experimental runs of each of two individual subjects and also the average correlations for all six subjects. You can scarcely ask for a better fit than the table shows.

Assumptions

The assumptions here, those needed and not needed, are almost the same as in the first two experiments. I will review them very briefly.

It is *not* necessary to assume the substitutability of persons. It *is* necessary to make the species assumption—that there are functions within persons that are the same for everyone. It *is* necessary to assume circular causation in the

Table 11.3
Correlations between Human Behavior and Model's Behavior

	Variable			
	Q_1	Q_2	H_1	H_2
Subject 1				
Run 1	.992	.971	.996	.995
Run 2	.983	.972	.989	.992
Subject 2				
Run 1	.968	.982	.986	.992
Run 2	.983	.972	.989	.992
Averages for six subjects				
Means	.979	.976	.990	.991

Note: See text for explanation of symbols.
Source: Excerpted from Marken (1986, Table 1, p. 273).

feedback loops. It is *not* necessary to count proportions of people who conform to the hypotheses; if one person does not, the experiment has gone awry. No tests of statistical inference are necessary.

The use of words is reduced to the simple instructions given to the subject; no words whatever were needed from the subject. By looking at the data, you can check whether the subject, every subject, is following the instructions. Indeed, when you see a subject behaving as in Figure 11.4, you do not need to assume that the subject understood the instructions or even heard them. You do not care.

The success of the experiment is not measured by the correlation between environmental input and action output. Instead, success is measured by the *lack* of correlation between environmental input (the random disturbances) and the controlled input (the perception of equal distances).

What Is Remarkable?

What is remarkable, I think, is the almost perfect fit between the behavior of the human subject (every subject) and the behavior of the computer model. That fit was achieved even though every subject had to cope with three random disturbances acting simultaneously, none of them ever repeated in a subsequent experimental run, and had to do so by using two hands acting independently.

It was achieved, too, even though a model had to be built that would act at two hierarchical levels and into which it was impossible to build a right answer for a way to achieve the equal distances, because the model (like the subjects) had to cope with unpredictable disturbances.

SELF-CONCEPT

Robertson, Goldstein, Mermel, and Musgrave (1987) carried out a series of experiments on the self-concept. I will recount four from among their experiments.

Procedure

In these experiments, the researchers gave students in college psychology classes 80 cards bearing adjectives describing personality characteristics. From the 80 adjectives, they asked each subject to pick 16 that they could confidently judge to be like them or not like them. They asked the subjects to sort the 16 adjectives into piles according to a Q-sort; that is, putting so many into the pile labeled "most like me" (one, actually, in this case), so many into the next pile, and so on, putting the most cards into the middle piles.

Once that was done, the students met in pairs. One student in each pair was labeled the "experimenter." Unbeknown to the other student (the subject), the "experimenter" in each pair had previous instructions. The "experimenter" looked over the subject's Q-sort, then read aloud the most-like-me adjective, and said, "No, you're not _____," pronouncing the adjective as the last word in that sentence. The "experimenter" then wrote down exactly what the subject said immediately after that.

Results

The researchers had postulated that all of us carry about self-images that act as internal standards in higher-level control systems. Like all higher-level standards, they argued, self-images tell lower-level systems the kinds of standards they should require of incoming perceptions. Since every subject had picked, from a large variety, his or her own most-like-me adjective, the researchers predicted that every subject would act to oppose the statement by the "experimenter." The statement "No, you're not_____" would threaten to disturb the self-image, and the subject would counteract the disturbance.

The researchers coded all the utterances of the subjects that the "experimenters" had written down. Robertson and his colleagues report four experiments conducted in this manner with a total of 35 subjects. They found only one utterance that did not seem to oppose the presumed disturbance. They found two utterances they were unable to code as opposing or unopposing:

```
Opposing utterances:        32

Unopposing utterances:       1

Uncodable utterances:        2

                        ------------

        Total subjects:     35
```

Assumptions

I think several features of the design worked out by Robertson and his colleagues helped the experiment to work well. First, in contrast to the researchers in the experiment I recounted in Chapter 4 under "Example," Robertson and colleagues did not pick out a particular dimension (intelligence, in that case) and assume that it would be in control for all subjects at the crucial moment. Instead, from a highly multidimensional collection of 80 adjectives, they asked the subjects to pick 16 they were able to say with some firmness of opinion were like them or not like them. That is, they allowed every subject to pick his or her own salient dimension. (A similar adaptation to individual standards was used by Dember, Earl, and Paradise in the experiment I told about in Chapter 9 under "Complexity" when they allowed each rat to pick the time when the runway with the stripes would become more "complex.")

Second, and again in contrast to the experiment in Chapter 4, Robertson and colleagues did not pick a particular kind of action to indicate opposition to the disturbance. The researchers in the experiment I told about in Chapter 4 demanded that their subjects counteract the threat to their self-images only by marking on a questionnaire their desire to read disparagements of intelligence testing. Robertson and colleagues gave no instruction whatever at the point when the subject's self-image was presumably threatened. They knew, of course, that the handiest use of the environment for almost all the subjects would be some utterance of words. Every subject, nevertheless, was free to choose his or her own use of the environment in counteracting the disturbance—whether words, hostile stares, expectorations, or punches in the nose. Actually, in writing about their coding, Robertson and colleagues mention only spoken words.

Third, Robertson and colleagues kept the self-image salient by allowing only a few moments between the Q-sort and "No, you're not_____" and by enabling the counteractions to occur only a split second later. The short times reduced the chance that some other high-level standard would come into play. The researchers in Chapter 4, in contrast, put six days between filling out the intelligence test and putting the presumed disturbance to the subjects, and then a good many minutes went by before the subjects could act against the disturbance. The researchers were, however, alert to the possibility that the subjects' governing standards might change. To mitigate that possibility, they reminded the subjects of the scores they had estimated they would get.

Fourth, Robertson and colleagues reduced to a minimum the use of language and therefore assumptions about the efficacy of communication. The "items" (adjectives) they used required no agreement about meaning between the subjects and the researchers or among subjects. In the experiment of Chapter 4, the items on the test had to have a meaning relevant to "intelligence" for subjects and researchers, and so did the subsequent tasks. In the experiment by Robertson and colleagues, however, neither the researchers nor other subjects needed to understand anything about how any subject sorted the adjectives. At the point of sorting, the only common understanding necessary was the understanding between researchers and subjects of the words "like you" and "not like you."

In the brief moments when the student "experimenter" said, "No, you're not _____" and the subject replied, the common understandings necessary were extremely simple. It was necessary for the "experimenter" to pronounce the subject's most-like-me adjective well enough so that the subject knew the "experimenter" was referring to that adjective, but the success of the experiment did not depend on anybody knowing what the adjective meant to the subject, the "experimenter," or the researcher.

Then the subject had to know that "No, you're not _____" meant that the "experimenter" did not agree with the subject's self-perception. Finally, assuming that the "experimenters" had copied verbatim what the subjects answered, the experiment depended on the researchers' agreement with the subjects on whether their utterances indicated acceptance or rejection of "No, you're not _____." The experimenters had to understand the subjects on nothing more subtle than that primitive dimension of acceptance or rejection.

Those comparisons show nicely the intimate connection between theory and method. Method that seems reasonable in input-output theory does not seem reasonable with a theory that assumes circular causation—and often vice versa.

The researcher accustomed to the traditional control-group design might complain that Robertson and colleagues did not test a control group. The logic of the control group is to see whether the predicted effect of the "independent variable" would occur without the "experimental treatment." That is, might the subjects have uttered a sentiment sounding like an opposition to "No, you're not _____" if the "experimenter" had *not* said that? What would the "treatment" in the control group be? Would the "experimenter" simply say nothing, waiting to see whether the subject spontaneously blurted something like "Yes, I am, too!"? Would the "experimenter" perhaps say, "Yes, you certainly are _____," and would the researcher count the frequency with which the subjects objected to the "experimenter's" agreement with them? I cannot imagine how a traditional control group could be designed for this experiment or what its use would be.

Robertson and colleagues admit that so far they have not achieved perfect results. They imply that they will continue to seek improvements in their methods, to which they refer as "primitive."

What Is Remarkable?

In the tracking experiments I described earlier in this chapter, it was easy to tell whether the subjects were controlling their behavior by a relational standard such as equal distances between symbols on the computer screen. When working with a high-level standard like self-image, however, and with words, it is not easy to be sure the high-level standard you are testing is always the one in control. Robertson and his colleagues did not track the maintenance of self-image over a number of minutes, but only at the one instant of the reply to the "experimenter." It would be very difficult to design an experiment that would track a particular high-level standard over a period of time, even a short period.

According to control theory, the person acts on the environment only when the maintenance of a standard is threatened and when the person can find an action that restores the desired perception. We can, therefore, see with some confidence a particular higher-level standard acting over a period of time to control perception only when the person can find counteractions to take during that period and when no standard at a still higher level takes charge during that period. In ordinary life, those conditions do not hold for very long periods except in situations the person experiences as stressful or in periods of severely focused concentration. To use stress in the laboratory to hold a high-level standard in place would be unethical, and to find fascinating activities that can draw severely focused concentration uninterrupted for some minutes is very difficult.

Considering those features of the high-level control of perception, I think the achievement of Robertson and colleagues—the "score" of 32 out of 35—is remarkable. It seems to me that several kinds of other high-level standards could have come into control in one or another of the subjects at the crucial moment when the "experimenter" said, "No, you're not _____."

One kind of standard other than self-image could have been something like, "I want to say something now that will please Dr. Robertson." A second kind could have been, "I want to be nice to my fellow student." A third could have been, "I want to protect myself against the possibility that this student and the professor are in cahoots to deceive me about something." A fourth could have been, "Part of my picture of myself is my understanding that other people do not always see me as I see myself. This person is entitled to his view of me. No comment is necessary." I cannot, however, imagine how these other standards could be predicted to produce a high percentage of statements in opposition to "No, you're not _____."

Experiments designed according to *S-O-R*, such as the one I recounted in Chapter 4, are always weakened by the influences of standards like those I just listed—standards experimenters ordinarily do *not* want to be in control. I think Robertson and colleagues showed great ingenuity in working out an experimental design that reduced to only 3 out of 35 the instances in which those unwanted standards apparently came into control.

Finally, I think it is remarkable how much Robertson and colleagues were able to reduce the degree to which the outcome relied upon agreement between researcher and subject about the meaning of words. We need more experiments designed to reduce reliance on semantic agreements. Of course, Robertson and colleagues must still rely on words to convey a picture of their experiments to you and me. I do not see any way out of that.

PREDICTING PARTICULAR ACTS

Now I can be more precise about what I mean by predicting "particular acts." For present purposes, I will ignore acts requiring only a fraction of a second, such as those that change the precise forces in muscles. It is true that those minutiae are indeed what the neural currents produce; they can produce nothing else. They cannot produce one of a class of acts. Classes exist only in our imaginations, not in the neural currents that produce muscle action. For practical purposes, then, to tell you what I mean by a particular act, I will skip over the minutiae.

The models in the experiments recounted here predicted very closely the types of acts the subjects would use to oppose the disturbances. The *countering action* was what the experimenters predicted. The researcher did not predict the moments or rates at which the subject would oppose the disturbance. That was impossible in the experiments using computers, because the disturbances occurred randomly. The researcher knew, too, that the subject would not always succeed in immediately counteracting the disturbance. (Indeed, one of the requirements of this kind of experimentation is that the measuring device—the computer—be able to measure changes in action more precisely than the human can accomplish them.) The researcher claimed only that the behavior of the human would be very close (with correlations like .98) to that of the model, errors and all, over some hundreds of moments.

Notice what the researcher had to know to test whether those continuing, uninterrupted, precise acts occurred. The researcher had to know, first, the internal standard each individual subject would seek to maintain. In the tracking experiments, the standard was one the subject adopted at the request of the researcher. Second, to calculate the accuracy of the results, the researcher had to be able to record the exact pattern of the disturbance. The researcher did not need to know the pattern in advance, but had to have a record of it after it had happened to be able to make the calculations. Knowing those two things, the researcher could make a prediction and present evidence.

Still, the experimenters did not actually predict particular acts—such as pulling back on a joy-stick or saying, "I am, too!" They predicted the *consequences* of acts. They predicted only that the subject would take *some* act to oppose the disturbance. It is true that a particular kind of act can indeed be predicted if opportunities in the environment are sufficiently restricted. It would have done the subjects sitting at the computers no good to shout, "Move left!" Perhaps some subjects did shout something like that, but to maintain their desired perception, they had to push on the joy-stick or push a key. The experimenters could predict that when the disturbance went one way, the subjects would move their hands to go the other way. In the experiment on self-concept, the environment was not quite as restricted. Not only could the subjects say anything that came into their heads, but they could give nonverbal responses. Judging from the report, however, all spoke words in addition to whatever else they did.

Ascertaining internal standards and tracking disturbances are much more easily done in the laboratory than in daily life. The subject in the laboratory can be requested to maintain a simple internal standard for a minute or two, and the subject's success in doing so will be documented in the data. In ordinary life, standards affecting action are multiple, and the effects of them become visible when (a) they are disturbed and (b) the person can see an opportunity for acting on the environment to restore them. At other times, the standards lie quiescent, so to speak. To predict action, a researcher would have to know, first, the internal standards that would be ruling in every individual at the times the environment would offer an opportunity to act on them. Second, the researcher would have to know whether the environment would disturb those standards. Third, the researcher would have to be able to record the continuing pattern of the disturbances the environment was putting upon each subject, not to mention disturbances arising within the subject. For practical purposes, that is asking a lot.

SUMMARY

I have recounted here four experiments built on control theory. The experiments illustrated a good many ways in which the method of specimens used with the assumption of circular causation, on the one hand, differs from the method of relative frequencies and linear input-output theory, on the other. I will not repeat here the differences described in the sections headed "Assumptions" and "What Is Remarkable." One feature of these experiments must surely impress social scientists: the insistence by these researchers that their data should fit *every* subject and their success in coming very close indeed to that goal.

12

Social Psychology

When I have written about behavior or theory in this book, I have usually written about the individual human. I brought in control theory because it illustrates so well what can be done with the method of specimens. If, following control theory, we take life's constant activity to be that of maintaining internal standards against threats from outside, then social life looms large, because other people comprise a very large part of the environment of most modern humans. Sometimes other people obstruct our purposes; sometimes they give us help. And often both at the same time.

The study of social life now becomes the study of the ways in which two or more people, all acting to maintain their perceptions according to their internal standards (purposes, goals, interests, values, and so on), sometimes find them disturbed by other people and sometimes find other people useful in counteracting the disturbances. The study of interaction among people becomes the study of overlapping feedback loops.

INTERACTION

From the viewpoint of control theory, an event or condition in the environment affects behavior if (and only if) the event disturbs a perceptual input the person is maintaining—that is, controlling. Everybody else, therefore, is simply a part of the person's environment and either a possible source of disturbance or a possible resource for opposing a disturbance. Sometimes another person is a help, sometimes a hindrance. That is not news.

Harmony

When, in pursuing our purposes, we make use of the environment (including other people) in such a way that we do not prevent others from using the environment in pursuing *their* purposes, harmony results. You and I can ride in the same bus even though I am going to the grocery store and you are going to church. You and I can work in the same surveying crew even though the chief thing I want is to make some money and the chief thing you want is to find out whether the Egyptian pyramids really do match well the proportions some archaeologist says they do.

None of us has wants, purposes, or internal standards about how every event should proceed. I may not care whether the bus goes down 12th or 13th Street to get to the corner of 14th and Lincoln. You may not care whether I take my day off from the surveying crew on Thursday or Friday. Coordinating and organizing is possible in social life, indeed, because so much of what goes on in the world about us interferes very little or not at all with our own purposes.

Conflict

Often, however, we do interfere seriously with one another's purposes. I use a piece of the environment in such a way that it closes off the use of that piece to you, and you cannot easily find some other piece to use in pursuing your own purpose. Then we are in conflict, as when we both want to go through a swinging door at the same time.

I will be writing, however, about conflict both between persons and within an individual. Therefore, to be clear, I will use "strife" to mean competing or opposing uses of a part of the common environment between two or more persons, and I will use "conflict" to mean opposing urges within an individual. Furthermore, I mean to exclude from my meaning of conflict those brief, temporary frustrations or puzzlements that recurrently and inevitably rise within us as we pursue our purposes—as we encounter temporary obstacles, circumvent them easily, and think no more about them. Ordinarily, when we encounter someone opposing us from the other side of a swinging door, one person gives way quickly, and both get through with hardly a flash of frustration.

Strife has a continuing effect between us only because of the conflict it engenders within us. When we cannot get through the swinging door, our individual purposes are frustrated. Though the frustration arises from the interaction between the two of us, the accompanying emotion and the urge to overcome or circumvent the frustration lies separately within each of us. And sometimes one of us finds that the obvious way to circumvent the frustration will threaten some other cherished internal standard. Maybe I want to perceive myself as a person for whom others ought to make way. Then, if I stand back from the swinging door to let you through first, I weaken my picture of myself. I do not want to do that. But if I get into a pushing contest with you, I delay getting to where I want to go. I do not want to do that, either. Doing either thing satisfies one internal standard or goal but violates another. As long as I insist on maintaining both goals unchanged or undelayed, I cannot satisfy either, my inner conflict continues, and so does the strife between us.

Strife continues between persons only as long as conflict continues within the individuals. When the inner conflict vanishes, so does the strife. If, as you are pushing on the swinging door, you suddenly remember that the appointment to which you are hurrying is not, come to think of it, for today, but for tomorrow, you no longer push frantically on the door. You stand back, and I barrel through. I no longer have a conflict, because I am now going on to where I want to go and at the same time maintaining my respect for myself. I do not carry on the strife; pausing to punch you in the nose would only delay me further. The strife could also be removed if I were suddenly to think that I could maintain my self-respect by verbal action instead of physical. I stand back and shout, "All right, all right! Come on! I'm in a hurry!" That shows you, I tell myself, that I am master of the situation—that I have not given in to your shoving, but have taken charge and ordered our movements to suit my own purposes. I have thus removed my own conflict and thereby the strife between us.

Another example: If you have an internal standard about making some money to feed yourself and family, and another about being nice to children, and the boss orders you to dump some toxic chemicals where children are likely to play, you have an inner conflict that can cause a conflict with the boss. If other jobs are readily available, the conflict, after some emotional upheaval, can be readily resolved. But if jobs are hard to get, the conflict hollows out a place for itself in your innards and sits there and gnaws.

At work, the action that follows upon a discovered conflict often reduces the conflict for some people (usually the bosses) but leaves it in place, or worse, for others. The boss says something like, "Yeah, yeah, I know you don't like it, but we've made the decision, and you're just going to have to live with it." The strife with the boss has not been removed; it has merely been pushed into the subordinate's belly, so to speak, where the boss hopes it will be invisible.

Inner conflicts do not go away just because the boss thinks it would be nice if they did. They do not go away until the person finds some way to restore the disturbed perceptual inputs. Sometimes employees do succeed in doing that without resorting to actions that harm the organization. At other times, however, distraught employees turn to irascibility, careless work, slow work, by-the-letter work, frequent absences, pilfering, ulcers, alcoholism, and sabotage. The conflicts have become visible again, but wearing different garments, and many people fail to recognize them, even those wearing the new garments.

The fact that interpersonal strife leads so quickly to *intra*personal conflict (and vice versa) makes it difficult to deal with. People often hide their purposes from others. Even when they do not try to hide them, they are themselves often unaware of them.

Treading on Feedback Loops

The key question for social psychology, it seems to me, is *whether an interaction of two or more people helps the participants to pursue their own purposes or hinders them* and the extent to which it does so. When another person interferes with your use of the environment, when the person chooses a path through the environment to use as a feedback function in such a way that you are prevented from using that path to build *your* feedback function, then the other person becomes a disturbance to your input. You must then act to oppose that disturbance. When that kind of interference comes about, one might say fancifully that the one person is "treading on the feedback loop" of the other.

The study of social life becomes the study of the ways that patterns of interaction do or do not lead people to tread on one another's feedback loops. When people can use the same environment, physical and social, in such a way that they help one another find feedback loops through the common environment, when they do not tread on one another's loops, then they find harmony, coordination, and productivity. When they use the environment in such a way that they hinder one another by treading on others' loops, then they find conflict, disarray, and ruin.

VARIATIONS AMONG ACTS

Under threat of disturbance to internal standards, we do not always choose particular acts or particular people with which to defend particular internal standards. There are many ways to skin a cat. That notion appears in some literatures as "equifinality." Until now, it has been the kind of concept that comes to naturalists after they have seen a pattern in many natural situations. The concept is at least as old as the adage about skinning a cat, but it has been an isolated and unshapely hypothesis that was unwelcome to most theorists in psychology, because it was still another nuisance that added "error" to research. Now, however, control theory derives this principle among its very first theorems. Variations among acts (in ways to skin a cat) arise from three sources.

Sources of Variation

First, we choose whether to act at all by whether an environmental event threatens to disturb some internal standard. That is the first source of variation in behavior. If an environmental event disturbs an internal standard, we act. If it does not, we do not. If the boss tells you that your lunch hour will now be from 11:30 to 12:30, and you do not have an internal standard that will be disturbed by that schedule, you say "OK," and that is the end of the matter. But if your conception of a proper schedule for nutrition, or your pleasure in meeting friends at noon, or some other match to an internal standard will be disrupted by the new lunch hour, then you try to dissuade the boss, start looking for another job, or take some other action.

The second source of variability in behavior comes from the means we choose (including particular people in the environment) to oppose the disturbance to the maintained perceptual input. The choice will depend (a) on what paths of action in the environment you think will be successful in opposing the disturbance. The profits in your business may be dropping. You may consider reducing the salaries of your employees. But you may judge that the productivity would then drop so much that the costs of operating would eat up the saving in salaries, so you reject that choice and try something else.

The choice will also depend (b) on whether an action will threaten your maintenance of some other internal standard. You may feel an obligation to pay "decent" salaries to your employees, and you may reject the choice of reducing their salaries because doing so would reduce your ability to carry out that obligation. The choice will also depend (c) on what you are capable of conceiving as a possible way to oppose the disturbance. You might not gather your employees together to ask them how profits might be restored, because that possible path of action might simply never come into your mind. Education and culture, among other influences, have a lot to do with what you will be able to conceive.

The third source of variability in behavior lies in the opportunities the environment actually offers. To satisfy a desire for sociability, nomads in a desert make use of places, occasions, and customs very different from those used by denizens of large cities in technologically developed countries. To get warmer, you can put on a coat—if you have one; you can build a fire—if there is firewood nearby; you can turn up a thermostat—if there is one in your building; you can complain to the building superintendent—if there is one.

The multitudinous ways humans use the opportunities in their environments to pursue their purposes are fascinating to anthropologists, archaeologists, ethnologists, sociologists—in fact to just about every "ologist" there is. But when we think with the *S-O-R*, we put on blinders that reduce our ability to see the astonishing creativity of humans in making use of their environments. Leona Tyler, in her wise and charming book *Thinking Creatively* (1983), writes about both equifinality and "multiple possibilities" and urges us not to think of ourselves as bound and predestined by our immediate circumstances. Read her book. You'll like it.

In sum, what people choose to do and with whom to do it depends, first, on whether an environmental event is threatening the maintenance of a perceptual input. Second, it depends on the things or people they choose with which to oppose the disturbance to the perceptual input. That choice depends on (a) the paths of action that seem likely to be successful, (b) whether the action chosen will threaten the matching of perception to some other internal standard, and (c) what they can conceive as possible actions in the environment. Third, what people do depends on the opportunities the environment actually has to offer. There is nothing profound about that. Football players, for example, know all about that sort of thing.

Simple though those ideas may be, they are very important in social life, and when we are busily pursuing our purposes, we often forget them. When we are living and working together with others, we forget, first, that others may or may not feel urged to act when we ourselves feel or do not feel the urge. And second, that others may or may not judge a path of action (a) likely to succeed, (b) likely to threaten other internal standards, or (c) likely even to be possible. And third, that the environments of other people may not offer the opportunities that our own offers to us. We may then set out upon actions that disturb other people's standards in ways that surprise us. And the less we are aware of those three sources of variation, the less able we are to cope with the surprises. Furthermore, if we are inept at communicating about these matters (and most of us, I think, are inept), the conflicts and mistakes are exacerbated.

Operational Definition

For several decades now, texts on methods in psychology and some other social sciences have made a big thing of the "operational definition." If you want to measure a certain variable, you can usually think of several ways to get indicators of it. You pick one set of events to observe and from which to take a measure, and then do your experiment. The one way you pick to make observations and measure your variable is called its "operational definition." When you use the notion of the operational definition, you must act as if the three sources of variation do not, in fact, yield variation.

In psychology, we say that we are working with two kinds of definition: the conceptual definition and the operational definition. The conceptual definition of the variable is what we would like to be measuring if only there were some real thing we could directly observe in its varying. The operational definition is the measurement we find it *convenient* to make. We say, "I am going to let the subject's pencil marks on this intelligence test be my operational definition of intelligence." Then we use our *conceptual* definition of intelligence to make predictions about the further behavior of the person who made those black marks. The conceptual definition, unfortunately, always includes many more kinds of acts in many more kinds of situations than making pencil marks on paper while sitting in a schoolroom.

The act or series of acts that enables a researcher to get a measure of a variable is subject to the three sources of variability I have described. Regardless of what a researcher would like a measure to measure, the behavior from which the researcher takes the measure can go one way or another because of any of those three sources. It is a wild hope that any one "operation" a researcher chooses can be showing some one thing to the researcher about all subjects and all environments. The operational definition is a terrible mistake. It has no magic to guarantee that all the subjects have chosen the same act for the same purpose.

Real Life

There is no such thing as real life. Or unreal life. That is, every condition or setting of human life is as real as every other.

In physical matters, the difference between the laboratory and "real life" is simply that the workers in the laboratory are usually more skillful (in the necessary ways) than those elsewhere and the tools more precise. Gold behaves the same way outside the laboratory as inside. So do hydrogen, arsenic, and chlorotrifluoromethane. Things balance in the same way, accelerate in the same way, and heat up in the same way in and out of the laboratory.

Similarly, people act to control their perceptions whether they are in the laboratory or out. As a natural kind, the person is as natural in and out of the laboratory as gold or arsenic. Both the experimenter and the subject in the experiment make use of the laboratory as an environment offering opportunities for building feedback functions in the same way that they make use of other environments. Laboratories, of course, offer opportunities different from those in other settings, and laboratories will disturb some internal standards that other settings do not, and therefore the particular acts (of both experimenter and subject) will be different. But in every place the person carries the same repertoire of perceptual inputs to be controlled—inputs that can be "disturbed"—and in every place the fact of hierarchical functioning remains, too. The relation between sound pressure and loudness (for a particular person) will remain the same in the laboratory and out. Maintaining the suitable visual pattern, a person will thread an automobile through traffic with the same capability for compensatory movement that Marken's subjects showed in maintaining an appropriate separation among the three lines on the computer screen. Job interviews, kaffeeklatsches, church services, football games, training simulations for corporate executives, and laboratory experiments all have their own realities.

Looking back, it seems obvious that people are people and that they carry their characteristics with them into the laboratory as well as elsewhere. Most psychologists, however, seem to have ignored that possibility until the 1960s. I can suppose only that the widespread acceptance of the *S-O-R* and linear causation persuaded them that people could be "controlled" in the laboratory or at least that the subjects' myriad purposes could be rendered harmless by randomization. Many psychologists seemed to be taken aback and surprised when the willfulness and purposefulness of humans in experiments was "discovered" in experiments and writings during the 1960s. Authors who come to mind are Edwards (1961), Orne (1962), McGuigan (1963), Breger and Ruiz (1966), Webb and others (1966), and Rosenthal (1967).

If only because every social setting offers a particular assembly of environmental opportunities, we cannot hope to generalize particular acts (uses of the environment) from one social setting to another. And because individuals have different hierarchies of standards, we cannot hope to generalize particular social acts from one person to another.

We mislead ourselves, however, if we think that lack of generalizability means an entire lack of predictability. Though the environment constantly changes, though social settings differ, though mixes of persons in social settings constantly change, though people have different hierarchies of standards, nevertheless social life retains a reasonable orderliness. How can that be?

Social life is orderly and predictable because all of us deal, in ordinary life, always with other individuals, not with large collectivities or masses or populations. When we say we are dealing with those large collectivities, we are actually dealing with inner images of them and with statistics about them. When we try to deal with them face to face, we can interact only with their leaders or their representatives—with individuals. When we deal face to face with a group, we are again acting in a common environment with other individuals. When we speak "to a group," we are putting sound waves into the air that are perceived by all those other individuals. The group does not have a single ear. It has as many ears, as many different ears as there are individuals.

We can gradually learn a good deal about the internal standards of the individuals with whom we deal, about what will disturb those standards and what will not. (I think we use some approximation of The Test that I described in Chapter 10 to do so.) Politicians, for example, learn early that all their constituents like to feel hopeful, but that they differ about the political actions they think will bring results to feel hopeful about. Accordingly, most politicians who speak to people via radio or television seem to prefer to say things that describe no specific intended action, but sound hopeful about whatever a listener may imagine fits into the politician's vague statements. We are aided in our learning (though sometimes hindered) by our common culture.

THE TEST IN EVERYDAY LIFE

In ordinary life, when we deal with other individuals, we look for ways to make their behavior reasonably predictable. To discover how we can anticipate the behavior of other individuals, we typically use an approximation of The Test that I described in Chapter 10. We look for the conditions in which the person pays no attention to what is going on, in which the person looks especially happy, and in which the person seems to be acting in opposition to something. From those evidences, we draw conclusions: "I think what she likes to see is. . . . " You might ask a friend about a mutual associate, "I wonder what's getting him all upset?" Your friend might describe some condition she thinks the associate might be finding it necessary to act against. And you might say, "But I can't see how he could even be aware of that." You would be applying step 7; you would be saying you cannot see how the person could be sensing that condition. But we rarely go systematically through all the steps.

The Test may seem to you time-consuming. It often is. Sometimes, however, the person is aware of the input quantity that is being disturbed, is aware of what is disturbing it, and is willing to tell you. In that case, The Test is very short: "What's bothering you, anyway?" And if the person's self-assessment is correct, you can run through the eight steps in short order.

With The Test, you can discover only what kind of disturbance will bring opposition from the person, and you can predict only that the person will do *something*. You do know that the person will do something immediately, even though sometimes the action the person finds suitable at the moment requires no muscular action at all. As to particular actions, you can usually rule out a good many for which the environment offers no opportunity. People will not use bulldozers to build a dam if they do not have any.

Using The Test may take a lot of detective work, but it is far more useful in working with individuals than the method of relative frequencies. With individuals, there are no relative frequencies. With the method of specimens, you learn something about a person with whom you have to work, for example, not something about presumed connections between stimuli and responses that depend on any of a hundred moderating conditions, and not something about 100 other people. You learn something about what will distract the person—what will draw off energies from the person's work into an effort to restore a disturbed perceptual input.

HIGHLY PREDICTABLE BEHAVIOR

The drugstore opens every day at the advertised time. Thousands of people drive mile after mile, day after day, with extremely few lapses, on the right-hand side of the road. Many highly predictable events, of course, become less predictable under certain conditions, but the conditions are often easily specifiable and widely understood. If you stand by a bus stop and wave at the bus, the driver will stop for you—except during the rush hour. The drug store will open at 9 o'clock every morning—except during an unusually heavy snowfall or after a sign has been put up reading "Going Out of Business." And so on. Many of the relative frequencies in ordinary life are so highly predictable that we are shocked if we find a relative frequency dropping below, say, 98 percent. No one in his or her right mind would advise us to quantify our confidence in the drugstore being open tomorrow morning by taking a random sample of observations. Why do social scientists not ask more often why it is that some actions are so predictable?

Would you recommend a person for employment if you were willing to bet 20 to 1 that he would show up for work more often than you could predict by flipping a coin? That is the kind of recommendation many social scientists make. It is true that some of them refrain from making such a recommendation to practical people. Some make it only to one another; that is, they claim that their willingness to make such a bet shows that they know something about what causes people to show up for work in the morning.

Social scientists using the method of relative frequencies jump up and down with joy when input-output correlations are large. "Look at that, $r = .87!$" they cry, or, "Look at that, $p<.001!$" Why, then, do psychologists not report studies of behavior where they know they can predict correctly almost all the time? Why do they not report the results of testing the hypothesis that the most likely next act of a person who has put the left foot forward is to put the right foot forward? That the most likely next act of a man who has shaved the left side of his face is to shave the right side? That a person who has finished the first course of a meal is very likely to sit there and start in on the next course? That a person who is addressed orally by another person is very likely to answer in some oral fashion?

I suppose one reason is that there is no glory in it. I suppose many psychologists would say, "Anybody can predict things like that. You don't need to know anything about psychology to predict things like that," or even, "That's trivial." Presumably a person who makes such a statement wants to predict things that will cause colleagues to say, "Gosh, you have to know a lot about psychology to predict a thing like that!" I suppose some psychologists might even complain that you do not need any theory to predict sequences of the sort I used for illustration.

My thought goes quite in the opposite direction. Surely, in a universe where entropy is one of the unquestioned facts of physics, negentropic events like highly predictable human behavior are the events that cry out for theory. Is it not amazing that the step of one foot is so reliably followed by a step of the other? It seems to me that the very predictability of routines like that should invite us to look for the marvels of internal organization that hold those routines in place. A few do try. Physiologists study homeostasis and sociologists study social control.

This puzzle fascinates me: In general, we should not try to predict particular acts of individuals. The environment is too changeable and the internal standards too various. Yet in ordinary, daily life, we find extremely regular patterns of behavior, so regularly repeated that we are astonished and even angry on those rare occasions when they fail. How do people maintain that constancy of action? And how do social scientists, most of them, maintain their continued avoidance of that question?

GOALS AND PURPOSES

Internal standards have the effect of what we call goals, purposes, attitudes, beliefs, desires, habits, ideals, ideologies, instincts, intentions, objectives, motives, needs, preferences, principles, readiness, skills, traits, values, wants, world views, yearnings, and so on. If I were to turn the pages of a dictionary, I could list here several pages of such words. Those criteria, those notions about what we want to happen to us, are carried in our individual brains. They exist only in neural nets—no place else. They cannot be observed directly. The existence of the corresponding controlling standards in the neural net can be inferred only by observing the kind of perceptual inputs that individuals act to maintain—as by The Test. Yet the social-psychological literature, and especially the social-science literature about organizations, is full of talk about the goals of groups and organizations.

Humans are able to adopt or borrow internal standards from others. They do so when they imitate the way someone else throws a ball or mixes batter, when they listen to someone describe the flavors of wine, when they learn to drive on the right-hand side of the road, when they learn not to invite black people or white people or Baptists to dinner, and when they learn how to defer to teachers and to bosses in a bureaucratic organization. Our culture makes it easy to adopt some kinds of standards and hard to adopt others.

Even when borrowed, no one's internal standard for controlling some perceptual input is exactly like another's. Every person is unique. Nevertheless, some internal standards are similar enough among enough people and are satisfied by those people enough of the time that they can coordinate their actions (build mutually helpful feedback functions) over extended periods of time. They can build roads on which almost everyone can be predicted to drive on the right-hand side almost all the time. They can paint the business hours of the store on the front window in the confident expectation that someone will be there in the morning to open the door and do business with the customers.

Borrowing internal standards—imitating and obeying—always has that yin and yang. On the one hand, each of us is unique, no internal standard stays "in charge" at all times, and sooner or later some member of a group or organization will substitute another internal standard for one the boss or the customer prefers. On the other hand, we can adopt similar enough standards so that daily business gets done, and a group of humans can sometimes act in very close concert, upon occasion almost as if the group had a single brain.

But as a collectivity or as a species, we are incapable of maintaining similar enough standards to avoid treading, sooner or later, on one another's feedback loops. We are incapable of maintaining coordinated action that is free for very long of contrary purposes and strife. No presumed "group goal" or "organizational goal" is maintained as an internal standard by any member uninterruptedly for a long period of time, and at any one moment only some of the members will be controlling their perceptual inputs with that borrowed standard. A group goal or organizational goal is a statement that somebody wants other people to adopt as their own internal standard, the proposer hoping that those other people will all adopt along with it the same meaning for it the proposer has. That is expecting a lot.

Systems

There is a lot of talk about "systems" nowadays. Sometimes writers seem to mean a procedure, simple (as a system for routing memoranda) or complex (as a "management system"). Sometimes they seem to mean an assembly of people, groups, and materials into a large organization (as a railroad system or a school system). Sometimes they seem to mean merely a reliable source of something (as a "support system"). Sometimes they seem to mean an organized body of thought (as a philosophical system).

An important idea in engineering, biology, and social science is that of a system as an organized unity with a boundary within which the whole is greater than the sum of the parts; that is, in which the rules describing the functioning of the parts are insufficient to describe the functioning of the whole. That idea has been adopted by many social scientists and imputed not only to individuals but also to groups and organizations. J. G. Miller's (1978) book *Living Systems* is an outstanding example of the latter.

To many people, especially many sociologists and social psychologists, what I am saying here will seem not merely brash, but heretical and even stupid. It will be especially unacceptable, I suppose, to adherents of the point of view that has acquired the label "living systems." Perhaps the two most widely known exponents of that point of view are Ludwig von Bertalanffy and James G. Miller, though they have many disciples. In Miller's 1978 book *Living Systems*, he says that cells are components of organs, organs of individuals, individuals of groups, groups of organizations, and organizations of societies. Furthermore, he says that all those are systems in the same sense: the same functions are performed within all of them, and the functions have the same relations to one another within all of them. The levels of system differ in the qualities and capabilities they have for coping with the external world, new qualities and capabilities emerging at each higher level.

Though I find much to admire in Miller's insights, I reject the pan-systemic view. I agree with Miller that people acting in concert (in groups or organizations) can do things beyond the capacity of an isolated individual. I do not agree that any arbitrarily chosen group or organization can act continuously to maintain a goal in the same way any arbitrarily chosen individual can do. Groups and organizations cannot have perceptions separate from those of their individual members, and therefore they cannot maintain purposes separate from those of their individual members.

It is true that members of a group can sometimes control their individual perceptual inputs according to an agreed goal as an internal standard for a short period of time. Athletic teams and theatrical companies are good examples. But that happens rarely enough that we gaze in admiration and delight when it does happen. Though I do not think groups or organizations "exist" in the sense of being a naturally found species or natural kind, I think the possibility of building a human group that acts like a system is an open question, a matter that should be investigated by the method of possibilities, a method I will describe in Chapter 13.

Be that as it may, the theory you have about groups and organizations as systems must affect the way you will use the method of specimens. If you think groups or organizations are species in the sense of showing invariants— ways of functioning that occur in every one of them—then you will study individual groups or organizations in the same way you might study individual humans. If, like me, you do not think groups or organizations are a species, you will study them as social environments that individual humans make for themselves in the pursuit of their individual purposes.

As one more argument for my point of view, let me remind you that if you want to study an individual thing as a member of its species, you must be able to recognize members of the species when you see them. I pointed out the difficulty of recognizing groups and organizations in Chapter 3 under "Groups and Organizations."

Serving Purposes

Let us give up imputing goals to organizations. Individual persons have goals; organizations do not. We can still, however, examine the human purposes organizations serve. We can still ask, too, about the effectiveness of an organization, or of organizing.

Every human organization is a part of the environment of some people—its employees, its suppliers, its customers, and its passersby. All those people use their environments—the parts of their environments that seem useful to them— as resources or paths through which to carry out their purposes. When it seems easier, more efficient, or more certain than using other parts of their environments, each of those persons—regularly, sporadically, occasionally, or maybe only once—uses the organization's activities, products, or physical plant as a means to carry out one or more purposes. Perrow says:

> Organizations are resources for a variety of group interests within and without the organization; they are used by a multitude of interests, and the announced purposes, while they must be met to some limited degree in most cases, largely serve as a legitimating device for these interests, or a mystification of the reality.
>
> There is nothing novel in the view that organizations serve many functions; what may be novel is to take this view so seriously as to put it at the center of our theory. . . . (1978, p. 106)

The "goals of the organization" are everything and anything and nothing, because "goals of the organization" focuses attention on the wrong thing: usually on the managers' imaginations and purposes instead of on the pursuit of purposes by all the people whose intertwined activities prompt us to say, *"There is an organization."*

When we ask what an organization does or ought to do, we inquire into the opportunities that various features of the organization offer to people who interact with other people in activities we connect in our minds with the organization. We find the organization doing some things that help or hinder some people in pursuing their purposes—things like making a profit or not, being a good or bad place to work, polluting the environment or not, providing more jobs or fewer, offering products of certain sorts and qualities, landscaping the grounds in one way or another, contributing money or not to civic projects, and so on.

Designing a harmonious organization is a matter of arranging materials and people and access to them in such a way that people can easily act while interfering with others' purposes very little if at all—that means everyone's purposes, not just the managers' purposes. It also means the purposes of people we do not ordinarily think of as "belonging" to the organization—customers, clients, suppliers, governmental regulatory agencies, the Sierra Club, the National Organization for Women, and other passersby. The various kinds of effectiveness to be found within the organization and in its neighborhood depend on that harmony.

Such a design is a tall order, but not as tall as it may seem at first thought. Remember that we do not care how every event proceeds. We do not, most of us, insist that everything proceed as we might design it. There is usually a lot of interpersonal slack. Indeed, we make a lot of conflict for ourselves and others when we make rules and specifications for events we really do not care about. There would be a lot more slack if we would give up telling other people how to do things when we do not really care whether they do them one way or another.

I am saying that organizations do not *have* purposes or goals; they *serve* the purposes of individuals. (That is really a one-sided way to say it; I will point out the other side later.) The mix of purposes an organization serves often changes, too, according to the demands of employees, suppliers, customers, and so on. Many schools now serve as day nurseries. On days of heavy snowfall, for example, when attendance will be low, many schools nevertheless stay open to receive the children of working parents who do manage to get to work and must drop off their children on the way.

Managers of business organizations sometimes do not put maximizing profit at the top of their priorities. Even when they keep profit ostensibly at the top of the list, they change the list of activities they charge off as operating expenses before calculating profit: making the plant a safer place to work, cleaning their effluents, beautifying their exhausted strip mines, and so on. Such changes, clearly, arise from the ways customers, neighbors, and passersby find that the activities of "the organization" are or are not helping them to pursue their own purposes.

Effectiveness

What, then, can we mean by "effectiveness"? Obviously, we cannot give an organization an overall measure of effectiveness except as an absurdly crude and arbitrary measure of a single feature or as an absurdly crude and arbitrary arithmetical average of features. An organization can beautify the community magnificently and go bankrupt. It can delight the stockholders and send most of its employees to the hospital with asbestos in their lungs. A few organizations succeed in making a profit, providing a healthy place to work, providing insurance against unemployment, providing day-care for children, and organizing the work so that almost all employees satisfy several of their deeper purposes through their jobs.

I like what Hackman (1985) and Aoki (1984) have to say about effectiveness. Here are Hackman's three criteria:

1. The productive output of the [individual, group, or organization] exceeds the minimum standards of quantity and quality of the people who receive, review, or use the output.

2. The process of carrying out the work enhances the capability of the [individual, group, or organization] to do competent work in the future.

3. The work experience contributes to the growth and personal satisfaction of the persons who do the work. (p. 129)

Here is a fourth that is my interpretation of Aoki:

4. Individuals have confidence that the work they do is helping to make their community, society, and even the world a good place to live in—for themselves, their grandchildren, and the people among whom their grandchildren will live.

But when I offer you my mix of Hackman and Aoki, I am not saying that there are four kinds of organizational effectiveness. There are as many kinds of effectiveness as there are purposes of individuals who interact with the people, products, or plant of the organization. I offer the four viewpoints listed above merely as an aid to getting away from the widespread view of effectiveness as return on investment, units produced per person-hour, percentage of students scoring above the national average on a standardized test, and the like. I offer them as a way of urging you to look in at least four directions for purposes the organization might be serving well or badly.

That is not the end of the matter. It is misleading to say (as I have been saying in many sentences here) that the organization does things that serve well or badly people's purposes. The phrase "organizational effectiveness" is misleading, because it implies that there is a thing, a delimitable entity, that we can call an organization and that it can, independently, act effectively or ineffectively in serving people's purposes.

Every human action is an interaction. I can say that an organization serves my purposes, or I can say that I make use of what the people of the organization do to further my purposes. Both ways of speaking about the interaction between me and some of the organization's people or products or services are partial and one-sided. If a customer finds that her electric drill does not work in a way to serve her purpose, that outcome is an interaction. It may turn out that the drill will work the way she wants if she turns the span-tab on the thring-casing. Did the organization fail to make the instructions clear enough, or did the customer fail to read the directions carefully? No one will ever know. All we can say is that there was an interaction between the way the instructions were written and put in the package, on the one side, and the customer's readiness, reading comprehension, and impatience to get on with the job, on the other side, that resulted in the span-tab's not getting turned. It is not an adequate conception to lay effectiveness wholly at the organization's door. Whether working conditions can be improved, for example, depends not wholly on the managers and not wholly on the union, but on the way the two interact (and on laws and other features of culture). In sum, effectiveness lies in the interaction, in the meshing, and the degree of effectiveness lies in the degree of ease or success with which people can carry out their purpose in that interaction.

I do not suppose many social scientists will be happy to look into those myriad interactions and purposes. We like one-dimensional measures that cover phantasmagoric complexities—such as Gross National Product, self-esteem, and salesmanship. You can always, of course, take averages of jumbles of particular effectivenesses. You can, if you wish, pretend that a hundred managers all have the same purposes and that a hundred workers all have the same purposes, though possibly different from those of the managers. But you will have to be satisfied with pretending.

On the other hand, I doubt that many managers will find my conception strange. Managing (like any other kind of human interaction) is a matter of being alert to the interactions with the physical and social environments that can serve as paths through which to maintain one's purposes. Though the manager's purposes may change slowly, the opportunities and threats that arise in the environment change more rapidly. The manager thinks about them one at a time, particularistically. The manager may say, "Oh, this is the kind of situation in which. . . ." But only at great risk does the manager go on to say, ". . . I can do the effective thing by applying recipe X without looking further into the details." Managers deal with particular employees, clients, and suppliers. Managers use measures of variables to give themselves hints about where to look for threats and opportunities, but their actions turn on the particularities of their interactions with other people.

To write here about the idea of effectiveness, I have used the doings of organizations to illustrate. The same arguments, however, can be made about the effectiveness of a policy, program, or routine within an organization. They can also be made about a feature of a culture. They are relevant to the work not only of organizational theorists and managers, but also of promoters of curricula in schools, of program evaluators, and of accountants.

Cooperation

In cooperation, the action of each person is a part of the feedback loop of the other. Both persons put shape on the immediate joint action. They must find joint action that will satisfy the internal standards of both.

Though the cooperative action on the group's task brings members closer to their individual goals, there are frequent periods during the coordinated effort when individuals must postpone the advance toward their individual goals. Waiting in line to buy a ticket is an example. Every one of the persons must judge that getting a ticket within a reasonable time and without getting torn clothes or a punch in the mouth will be better done by standing in line than by fighting to get to the window immediately. Cooperating requires every person, for a time, to put a certain kind of internal standard above his or her own individual goal, even though the person is cooperating for the purpose of achieving that individual goal. The internal standard that must rule in all the persons is an internal standard *for cooperating*.

In a group in which all members are guiding their joint work by the superordinate standard of cooperation, the members are arranging and scheduling their use of the common environment so that they do not tread on one another's feedback loops. They are dovetailing their loops in such a way that one person's use of the environment to accomplish the task also moves the others along in their efforts to accomplish it. Because of that interlacing of feedback loops, I like to put the label "loopy group" on a collection of people such that every member is maintaining an internal standard for cooperating with every other member in respect to at least one task.

A group can never behave exactly like an individual's neural net, because every component (person) in a group contains its own neural net and acts willfully. Nevertheless, given a strong norm of cooperation and clear task goals, it is possible for limited periods of time, and deeply gratifying, too, for humans to coordinate their actions almost as harmoniously as an individual's neural net coordinates the muscles of a body. If you are in a doubting mood about this, take time out and go watch a ballet.

A few loopy groups have been produced by design and documented. A remarkable piece of work, and one of the earliest well documented, was the transformation of hostility into cooperation between temporary boys' groups at Robbers Cave by Sherif and company (1961). Richard Schmuck and I have aided the formation of a few groups embedded in school districts that show all the marks of strong loopiness and have exhibited unusual durability; one is thriving after 19 years. Some of the less formal documentation of those groups appears in Schmuck and Runkel (1985, pp. 463–500). As to organizations, I do not think that any "species" of organization now exists, nor that any is likely to be produced, at least not soon. It would be an astonishing achievement if, some fine day, someone would discover how to build organizations such that a series of them functioned with the same invariants. I do not now, however, see how that could be done, and if you force me to make a pronouncement, I will say that it is impossible in principle.

You might be wondering whether I am saying that it is a waste of time to try to study organizations. No, I am not saying that. You can study individuals and groups *in* organizations—the way they organize and make use of the social and physical environments we call "organizations." Beyond that, you can study what people who organize themselves *can* do instead of studying what they *do* do—a matter to which I will return in Chapter 13.

CONTROLLING OTHERS

For decades, a large topic in social psychology has been that of the influence of the group on the individual. That is an *S-O-R* conception: put the individual in a social environment in which people are doing or saying so-and-so, and think of that environment as an input. Then predict that the individual will yield an action output of thus-and-so. Managers and organizational theorists have felt the enticements of that conception. When taking action to maintain a desired perceptual input, however, people often show an astonishing ingenuity. When we think their courses of action are obviously *A* or *B*, we are often surprised to find them choosing *C* or *D*. People who want the behavior of others to be highly predictable find human ingenuity annoying.

We often try to make the behavior of others more predictable by restricting the opportunities for action in the environment. We often try to put fences of one kind or another around people—fences within which only the actions we prefer will be available. In prisons, we use barriers beyond the physical ability of the prisoners to overcome—stone walls and iron bars. We also use barriers that soak up the energy of people who try to fight their way through them. If you have to go through five secretaries and five underlings to get to the president, waiting a month or two for each appointment, you are likely to give up from sheer emotional exhaustion. People have written dramatic books, detailing the years of effort and the harassment along the way, endured by employees of the U.S. government who tried to get the attention of someone several levels above them in the bureaucracy. We also erect obstacles by making arrangements we think will be beyond the ingenuity of others to penetrate, as when we hide candy from a child or information from a competitor or when we write an agreement in language that only people with special training can understand. Lawyers, tax consultants, and consumers' advocates are kept busy helping people find their way through this kind of barrier.

We also use rewards and punishments. We try to coax more selling with awards to the Salesperson of the Month. We threaten employees with admonitions not to do anything beyond their job descriptions. We give gold stars and merit badges to children and awards and bonuses to adults. We threaten every-one with thousands of laws that specify what the courts and the police might do to them if they transgress.

Trying to construct an environment that is proof against human ingenuity has two flaws. First, there is no end to patching the fence. Other people are always more clever than we think. We must continually make our walls thicker, our difficulties of access more devious, our incentives more frequent, our threats more omnipresent. Second, restrictions, discouragements, deceptions, incen-tives, and threats all create conflict. Consider punishment and threat, for ex-ample. "Punishment" is punishing when we believe the person doing it to us intends to go on preventing us from getting what we want. Since the acts we were using before the punishment were maintaining the input we wanted, we are now in conflict within ourselves. Allowing the punishment to continue vi-olates the standards that tell us the punishment is punishing. But to give up the previous acts violates the standards we were maintaining with them. That in-ternal conflict diminishes our effectiveness, if not worse.

When internal conflict arising from interpersonal action (punishment) is not resolved quickly, it easily spreads. Our society is already so full of threats of punishment that another threat can easily reduce the degrees of freedom in using a mutual environment to the point where a number of people find that all the ways they might use the environment result in strife. Threat breeds more threat, more conflict, more anxiety, more effort wasted in fighting off threat, more neurosis, and more violence.

Consider reward. Let me get out of the way, first, that I am not using the word here in the sense of "a rewarding experience" such as an esthetic plea-sure or a goal achieved. I am using it in the sense of an incentive given in the attempt to control behavior. A reward has its effect only if there is a good possibility that you will not get it. A good thing that happens in the natural course of events, like warm weather or letters from friends, is not a "reward" in the sense of an incentive; it is merely one of the good parts of life. A reward limits behavior only if it is accompanied by the threat that it might be withheld. Rewards intended as incentives are always accompanied by the proviso that you get them only if you do what the other person wants. A reward, in other words, is a way of setting up a threatened punishment. I have already explained about threats and punishments.

Many people speak as if *I* can motivate *you*, as if motivation is something one person does to another. If you are hungry, and I put a dish of food in front of you, have I motivated you? If you are not hungry, and I put the food in front of you, do I cause you to act? If you are not hungry, and I lock you in a room for 24 hours without food, have I done something to cause you to act? Act how?

The internal standard for hunger is there all along, eating or not. When I put food in front of you, I make it easier for you to use one path through the environment instead of another. When I lock you in the room, I make it hard for you to use any path except calling out for food (or maybe pressing a lever, if that is part of my experimental design). I cannot do anything in either case about motive. I alter the ease of finding one kind of feedback loop or another. That is all I can do.

The idea of controlling other people stems from the conception of the *S-O-R*, and the search for more effective ways of controlling other people is carried out almost entirely with the method of relative frequencies. That is natural, since a great many people are looking for ways of controlling large numbers of anonymous people. When, however, we study individuals with the method of specimens, the enterprise of controlling other people comes to seem misconceived, hopeless of much success, and extremely expensive—as penologists and some lawmakers have discovered.

SUMMARY

The essential characteristic of the method of specimens is that of looking for invariants in the functioning of individuals. That kind of search has immediate implications for the study of social psychology. The basic implication is an old idea that is nowadays often forgotten; namely, that the social psychologist must know the requirements of individual functioning to be able to know what to predict—and what not to try to predict—about interaction among humans. Krech and Crutchfield, whose insights I think have yet to be surpassed, wrote this in 1948:

> But we must constantly remember that when we treat the group as our unit of analysis and seek to discover laws of group behavior, we cannot merely substitute the word "group" for the word "individual" in valid psychological laws and assume that we now have equally valid laws of group dynamics. Every time we change our unit of analysis we must beware of ascribing to one unit the properties that are meaningful for the other unit. . . . [W]ithout independent verification, the laws of interpersonal relationships, for the individual as our unit, cannot be taken over and applied to inter-group relationships for the group as our unit. (p. 21)

According to control theory, I think, the key question for social psychology is the extent to which a social interaction helps the participants pursue their own purposes, or hinders them in doing so. More technically, the question is that of the ways individuals can use a common physical and social environment and, while doing so, maintain the necessary degrees of freedom so that every individual can avoid inner conflict.

People act to control their perceptions whether they are in the laboratory or elsewhere. If you are using the method of specimens to study the ways feedback loops and control hierarchies work, you have few of the worries about experimental "controls," intervening variables, and so on that lead the user of the method of relative frequencies into the unending slicing I described in Chapter 7.

A rich field for investigation receiving little attention nowadays is that of explaining how the many, highly predictable regularities of everyday life are maintained.

An implication of control theory is that we should give up looking for "group goals" and "organizational goals." The one exception is the possible adoption by every individual in a group, for a limited period, of cooperation itself as a superordinate internal standard.

Attempts to "control" particular acts of other people lead immediately to lowered productivity and before long to conflict and violence.

V

Other Methods and Summary

I have devoted this book to two methods of research—two methods of getting information that helps us get ready for future experience. I have argued that most social scientists—and most of the rest of us, too—expect the method of relative frequencies to deliver a kind of information it cannot deliver. As the right alternative, I have described the method of specimens.

Those two methods cover a vast amount of information-getting. They do not, however, cover everything. I agree with Lindblom and Cohen's (1979) book about Professional Social Inquiry. They tell how PSI (of which academic social science is a part) is only one of many ways of getting useful knowledge and can be no more than that. Also useful, they say, are ordinary knowledge, social learning, and interactive problem solving. But though I agree with them, I naturally prefer my own categories. In Chapter 13, I will describe action research and what I call the method of possibilities. Chapter 14 will summarize everything.

13

Action Research and Possibilities

Most books on social science portray generalizing as turning one's attention from a smaller number of people in a sample to a larger number of people in a population. That kind of generalization is useful in casting a net. If, however, we want information generated from research to be useful locally, with a particular organization, group, or person, then generalization must go the other way—from what is true of a lot of people to what is true of these few or this one.

GENERALIZING

Research, at least some research, should give us some information useful later, outside the research setting. It should help us get ready for future events.

Sometimes in research, formal or workaday, we observe a few instances and extrapolate from them. We get ready for a lot of later instances by supposing they will be similar to the lesser number of instances we have already experienced, as in observing a sample from a population. We go, that is, from the particular to the general. At other times, we observe a lot of instances and generalize from them to the very next particular instance about to happen. So it is when we study trends in the stock market and then purchase particular stock, and when we study the scientific literature on managing organizations and then start up a series of "quality circles" in our own company. We go, that is, from the general to the particular.

When we act, we must always act *as if* some narrow range of conditions exists. (Actually, we almost always act as if several, maybe a multitude of, particular conditions exist.) When we walk, we act as if we will discover the foot meeting the ground or the step at about a certain place. We prefer to act as if the error we will encounter between our internal standards and what we perceive will be small and easily corrected—as it is, for example, in the thousands of small acts we take every day in walking.

In social science, a hypothesis enables us to anticipate a sufficiently narrow range of experience (observations) so that we can make sense of it and act in a way that carries forward our purposes. In daily life, a "hypothesis" or anticipation does the same thing, though we may put it into words only vaguely or even leave it entirely unconscious, and though we may not always be thorough in noting the relevant later experience. Generalizing, whether or not we are social scientists, becomes useful when it narrows anticipation sufficiently that we find it easy to adapt to the range of unpredictability that remains. In most actions in daily life (though I cannot say I know how to count actions) we do anticipate very well. The map in our heads for getting to the grocery store sufficiently reduces the errors we will make so that we get there easily even through varying patterns of traffic and even when we have to detour around street repairs.

The anticipations of social science, however, often help us little in daily life. It is not very helpful in ordinary life to be correct in a statistically significant proportion of trials. If daily life were no more successful than that, we would be losing our way to the grocery store so often and find our feet meeting the ground at the wrong times so often that civilized life and probably life itself would be impossible. Not only does the method of specimens do better than that, but so do action research and the method of possibilities.

ACTION RESEARCH

Action research mixes research and consulting. Its methods amalgamate the methods of relative frequencies and of specimens. Social psychologists like to give Kurt Lewin credit for originating the method, and I have no doubt that he made many psychologists and sociologists more conscious of method when they set out to give people practical help than they otherwise would have been, and I have no doubt also that he enabled many to see the continuity between the laboratory and other realms of life. But getting useful information at the same time that you are consulting with people about how to get things done in a more satisfactory manner is surely as old as language.

Agricultural extension agents engage in action research when they help farmers try a new technique or a new seed, help the farmer learn to record data (both botanical and social) systematically, and report the results to other farmers so that experience can be cumulated. Curriculum consultants engage in action research when they help a group of teachers design a new curriculum, help them learn to collect and record data from students, teachers, parents, and administrators, then help them revise their curriculum and procedures, and report the results (educational and social) to other workers. And so on.

Stuart Cook, one of those who helped action research to become a conscious method, knows a lot about the history of it. Here are a few of his sentences:

> it [is] clear that during the mid-1940s, action research developed independently in a variety of disciplines. Among them were group work, education, industry, and . . . community development among American Indian tribes. . . . Out of this came the action research aspiration—the goal of conducting studies that advanced both scientific principles and social change.
>
> The last decade has seen a vigorous revival of interest in action research. This may be observed in the fields of organizational development, education, public administration, community psychology, and program evaluation. By contrast, a look at contemporary academic social science suggests that Lewin failed in his effort to persuade colleagues that knowledge of people and events could best be acquired by learning how to change them. (1988, p. 2)

Consultants differ among themselves and so do researchers in whether they choose to call some particular activity action research. Cook's phrase about advancing both scientific principles and social change is about as close as a lot of people will come to agreeing on a string of words they consider equivalent to the label "action research." To me, the core features of action research are undertaking some sort of change to answer the purposes of some people in a natural situation, entering the undertaking with some explicit ideas about what will work, keeping careful records of events, inspecting the data periodically for evidence of the usefulness of the ideas, and being explicit—at some point when something useful seems to have been achieved—about the serviceableness of the original ideas. Those intentions and actions can occur on the part of the consultant-researchers, the local participants in the change, or both— preferably both. People in organizations can also engage in action research by themselves without the help of outside consultants or researchers.

Investigators, consultants, and counselors who concentrate on the dynamics of one-to-one interaction sometimes look upon the use of the method of relative frequencies, when applied to the conduct of everyday life, as offering information that is too thin to be used in practical situations, as too slow for the information to be used anyway, and, when you come right down to it, as being pretty close to charlatanism. Investigators, consultants, and evaluators trained in the current lore of relative frequencies sometimes look upon information got from the one-to-one encounter as ungeneralizable and therefore not really information anyway, as too fleeting for it to be used, and, when you come right down to it, as being pretty close to charlatanism. Some people do practice charlatanism, but they do so because they wish to deceive, not because a methodology has led them to it. I hope it is clear that I respect both methods and their users. People who have worked with action research find that blending the two methods and letting their activities alternate between them is far more useful to consulting and to getting information that is useful for further consulting than using either method alone.

Even though almost all action researchers and consultants have so far (to my knowledge) carried out their research with the method of relative frequencies as their conscious guide to the "research" side of their work, I think the efficacy of action research comes from three features that actually arise from the mixing of the two methods.

First, action researchers try to run their cycles of collecting data and drawing conclusions from them faster than the cycles of work in the organization where they are consulting, or at least faster than opportunities for change arise. The frequent data collection by both researcher and client and their sharing of the data enable both researcher and client to keep track of changes in the population—that is, among the members of the organization.

Second, action researchers, whatever they may say, actually pay little attention to operational definitions. They are alert for any auguries they may happen upon that can give them clues to the readiness of participants to move in a new direction. They use data not only from formal questionnaires and interviews, but from informal conversations, memoranda and other daily and weekly documents, events they come upon or hear about, the behavior of participants during training, and so on. The result is that they get much more accurate pictures of the kinds of events people will act against as they approach points of change.

Third, action researchers look constantly for auguries of motivations that are being satisfied or frustrated in the daily life of the organization. Whatever the conceptions of motivation the action researchers may have, that alertness enables the researchers to form opinions about working conditions in which people feel unstressed and can devote their attention to work. It also enables them to form opinions about stressful conditions in which participants must take time out to counteract the stresses. Action researchers watch for auguries of motivations of key people and for auguries of common motivations within groups. As a result, they are able to alter their data collection as they go along to assess the variables (or note the auguries) that the participants choose as fateful and to modify or replace the variables they, the researchers, chose at the outset. As it turns out, researchers who violate the canons of the method of relative frequencies often use tactics that approximate The Test.

Diagnosis

The method of relative frequencies and data generated in previous studies by that method are useful in making informed guesses about the environmental conditions (both physical and social) in which the current clients are embedded and about the feedback functions they will choose most frequently—about the methods of dealing with the environment their training and their culture have persuaded them are effective or efficient. The method of relative frequencies can tell consultant and client about the likely distributions of those conditions and habits. Consultants and clients can anticipate better what to be ready to cope with.

But no matter how many hypotheses or hints we may take from research done by the method of relative frequencies, we still have to diagnose. We still have to ascertain the levels of conditions or the values of variables existing in a particular situation, and we still have to test for the internal standards of particular people, so that we can judge how useful those hypotheses and hints may be. Competent consultants, using the knowledge they have about human behavior in organizations, go in with tentative hypotheses about what might be going on. Then, working together with the clients, they collect data not only at the beginning of the consultation, but repeatedly, from individuals, dyads, groups, interfaces, and the organization as a whole, changing the hypotheses and the courses of action to suit—again working jointly with the clients.

Risks

That procedure is quite contrary to the instruction most methods books give for rigorous research. But it is one thing to cast a net to make a catalog of current behavior and quite another thing to undertake change in human affairs. When we invite people to take new action, we are asking them to take risks. We are asking them to try out paths through the social environment that would not have been their own unaided first choice and to wait sometimes a long time to discover the wisdom of their action.

In natural social settings, we can never predict in enough detail how a planned new course of action will go. The participants and the consultant must be ever alert to detect disturbances that are not quickly reduced—disturbances that bring conflict and therefore wasted effort. Participants and consultant must then hunt for actions that will enable everyone to find nonconflicting ways of reducing their disturbances. When we set off change in an interlacing network of feedback loops, it will never be enough to change a few variables and then sit back and watch—unless we are remarkably hardhearted.

Examples

Here are two quick examples of action research.

City Employment Services. Kaplan, Lombardo, and Mazique (1985) report a project that illustrates how research and consultation can meld. They called the client organization the "City Employment Services" or CES. The agency had been established to provide employment training and work experience to the unemployed. But the local and national economy was threatening the agency with program cuts and layoffs, and there were serious conflicts among the top three layers of the agency—the 17 managers who were the actual persons with whom Kaplan, Lombardo, and Mazique would consult.

The agency director had heard about an organizational simulation (a training game) called the "Looking Glass" from one of his department heads who had participated in it. The director invited the consultants to perform the simulation with his 17-member management team. After some hours with the director alone, the consultants met with the director and his three department heads. The department heads were dubious. The consultants met next with the 12 members of the third layer of managers. They were even more dubious.

Instead of going into the simulation, the consultants offered a preliminary diagnosis as a trial activity. Because the members of the management team seemed to want some immediate results from whatever the consultants did, the consultants also designed the diagnosis to lead to some action. Their report described the diagnosis:

> The preliminary diagnosis took the following form. . . . (a) confidential interviews with each member of the team and limited observation of the team in meetings, (b) a questionnaire . . . , and (c) a skeletal report offering tentative generalizations about the team—with no individuals identified—supported by quotations from the interviews and a series of meetings to discuss the validity and implications of the report. . . . We [had] interviewed [every] person and obtained a 100 percent response rate for the questionnaire. . . . (pp. 244–45)
>
> During the [series of meetings to discuss the report], . . . we challenged the team to undertake a breakthrough project aimed at one important problem.
>
> From the long list of complaints, the CES management team . . . chose to focus on a current problem of the agency: disciplinary action, such as that directed at tardiness and poor attendance, and the inconsistency with which it was taken. They designed a simple structure for solving the problem, including a timetable and system of accountability. Included in the team's project was the agency director's personal breakthrough goal, which was to stay in regular contact with the committee and hold it accountable for orderly and timely progress toward its goal. . . . The project thus provided the team an opportunity to break out of the rut that had demoralized it. (p. 246)

After the team got going on its "breakthrough project," its members also agreed to undertake the Looking Glass simulation. The exercise took three days, the first day with the Looking Glass simulation itself, the second to "dissect their experience," and the third connecting the experience to their regular work and planning changes.

> We collected data on the team's experience in three ways. First [two observers] observed [each "division"] closely . . . and took copious notes. Second, . . . participants filled out standard questionnaires on what had been accomplished and [how it had] occurred. Third, in the sessions held after the Looking Glass simulation, data were elicited from the participants [in] discussions. . . .
>
> The brunt of the work on individual learning was done in the afternoon session of the second day, when participants each had a half hour or more to learn what

other members of their divisions thought of their behavior during the Looking Glass simulation. This type of session allows people who actually work together to draw on both their work experience and their Looking Glass activities. (p. 247)

You can see in those paragraphs the interplay between gathering anonymous data and helping individuals to find what it was they really cared about.

Cadres of Organizational Specialists. In 1968, Richard Schmuck and I, with a dozen assistants, began a project in organizational development with a school district in the Northwest containing twelve elementary schools, three junior high schools, and two high schools. The district was growing very rapidly, and new administrators and old were tripping over one another's feet—and their feedback loops.

We collected a great deal of relative-frequency data, eventually finding ourselves, after four years, analyzing data from thousands of questionnaires and hundreds of interviews. The questionnaires and interviews did not retain the same items from cycle to cycle. We kept changing the items as we discovered new things we and our clients needed to know about.

The story of that project and its "results" in statistics are given by Runkel, Wyant, Bell, and Runkel (1980). Here I want to say only that enabling people in the workaday world to change their ways of coordinating their efforts does not come from long-distance predictions with statistics. It comes from providing people with better ways of anticipating what their individual colleagues will find to be disturbances and with ways to take joint action to reduce the disturbances.

In any consultation of any length, consultants and participants will find themselves coping with unforeseen environmental changes. For example, the effects of nationwide political turmoil and educational change were evident as we began training school staffs in the fall of 1968. First, much of the administrators' energy was devoted to forming policies that would lessen the pressure put on them by the more conservative segment of the community. Second, the district launched a number of innovative programs that affected our work. Meanwhile, the area's economic boom continued at a feverish pitch, although signs of an impending collapse began to appear by mid-year. The research we did was not what anyone would call a "controlled" study.

We wanted to leave behind us new capabilities among the school personnel. The way we chose to do that was to establish a "cadre of organizational specialists" to become organizational consultants to their own district. They turned out to be remarkably successful. In fact, they did better as consultants than we ourselves did. By the time we began our second cadre, in a district about twice the size of the first one, we had formulated ten rules by which we thought a cadre should work. Here are some of them, quoted from Schmuck and Runkel (1985, pp. 465–66):

1. Draw members from all ranks and from throughout the school district.

2. Assign members part-time to the cadre.

. . .

7. Train the cadre to provide services through temporary *teams* drawn from its membership. A cadre member should consult alone only in exceptional circumstances.

. . .

10. Provide time for the cadre's own self-renewal: recruiting and training new members, distributing information about the district among members, acquiring new skills, renewing the cadre's cohesiveness, planning for the future.

You can see that those rules encourage a lot of face-to-face interaction of cadre members throughout the school district—a lot of opportunity to learn about purposes of individuals and their disturbances. Furthermore, they demand that cadre members learn a great deal about one another as individuals.

That joint use of one another's resources and resourcefulness in finding ways to make use of the social environment to further personal goals and purposes while maintaining "organizational" goals—that cooperation in the loopy group, in short—is what we think has made cadres so welcome to colleagues in their school districts and what has given them their longevity. The welcome and the longevity do not come from the right formal organization or the right leader or the right amount of money or any other "right" input. They come from willingness and skill in finding joint feedback loops through the environment.

There again, the work went back and forth between the two methods. The work that left a continuing capability behind, however, was done with the method of specimens.

Summary

Action research mixes research and consulting. It makes use of both the methods of relative frequencies and specimens, of both formal and informal research, and of both conscious and unconscious generalization.

Action researchers try to run their cycles of data collection and conclusion-drawing faster than the cycles of the clients' work, or at least faster than the appearance of opportunities for change. They are alert for auguries of the readiness of participants to move in a new direction. They look for clues about the kinds of events people will act against as they approach points of change.

Diagnosis is always necessary in the natural setting. Change in the natural setting, however, is risky, and clients want to know what they can count on from their immediate individual colleagues, not what the probabilities are from a statistical analysis.

Accounts of action research and organizational development appear frequently in the *Journal of Applied Behavioral Science*, in *Organizational Dynamics*, and in other journals. A couple of recent writings on consulting that I admire greatly are two by Weisbord (1987a, 1987b).

POSSIBILITIES

I think most people devoted to the method of relative frequencies have failed to appreciate the usefulness of the single trial. The single case has been described by most people who write books on social-science method as yielding not much more than a single data-point that must be put together with more data-points before any useful conclusion can be drawn. But a single case can be a trial, a demonstration that a thing widely thought to be unlikely can indeed be brought about.

If you wonder whether a coin will turn up more heads than tails, it is true that one toss is not going to tell you. That is a question that can be answered only by the method of relative frequencies. Often, however, we want to know not the relative frequency with which something happens, but whether it can happen even once. When we want to know that, one successful trial can answer the question. If you wonder whether your tire has a slow leak, one immersion in water will tell you. If you want to establish bus service across the Great Sandy Desert of Australia, one run will probably not tell you how well you will be able to maintain schedules and how much your monthly repair bills will be, but if you get across the desert on your first run, you will then know that it is *possible*. Thor Heyerdahl's voyages in craft made of balsa and of reeds, built as much like those of some thousands of years ago as it is possible to ascertain, demonstrated that it was possible for those early people to traverse the ocean routes Heyerdahl did.

Of what use was the first voyage of Columbus or the first rocket to the moon? Those ventures did not tell people all the difficulties that would be encountered in later voyages, but they demonstrated what was possible, and they confirmed a lot of the ideas the voyagers had about what was required to get there. At the very least, they disconfirmed a lot of dire predictions made by opponents before the trips were made.

If you think your gladioluses are going to grow to about three feet high, which is about what everyone else expects, one gladiolus is not going to prove you right or wrong about your whole bed of gladioluses. Everyone will say, and properly, to wait until some more grow up before you calculate their average height. But if you say that you have one seed that will produce a gladiolus ten feet high, and people say that's absurd, but it does, then people ought to pay attention.

Flukes

Whether one trial is worth attention depends on whether other people say you can achieve what you are setting out to achieve. If you demonstrate that something is possible, and people say, "Oh, it was just a fluke," then whether they are justified depends on how likely a fluke can be. If you are tossing a coin, a fluke occurs easily. Every toss is a fluke. If you cross the Great Sandy

Desert in a bus, you may have been lucky, but it was not a fluke. Your bus *did* have the transmission and the tires and the air cleaner to enable you to make the journey. You did have a map that would guide you across. You did not overestimate your physical stamina. And so on.

Look back at Figure 10.2. In the lower right corner, you see a box labeled "Events irrelevant to actor." That box stands for the side-effects of the action the person chooses through which to carry out a purpose. You walk through a room to reach another one. You leave the air a little richer in carbon dioxide. You leave a smudge of dirt on the rug. Though you walk through the room to serve your purpose, you cause changes in the environment that you do not intend, that you do not care about, and of which you are usually not even aware.

A school principal tells a teacher he is assigned to room 213 next term. The principal's purpose, let us say, is merely to transmit that information so that this teacher will meet his class in the right place next term. The perception the principal wants to bring about is seeing every teacher in an assigned room on the first day of the new term. Other effects of the principal's utterance may be that the teacher feels lowered in status because room 213 is in the old part of the building, feels worried because the number ends in 13 and is therefore unlucky, and begins to hunt in his mind for some way to change his assignment. Later, when the principal becomes aware of those side-effects, she may say to someone, "By some fluke, I assigned that room to a teacher who was superstitious about the number 13." Every act has its side-effects. But every act is purposeful, too.

All "case studies" in social science are complex, and they all deal with acts having purposes. They are not tosses of a coin. The interdependencies of people in their common environment are full of occasions when things can go wrong, as full of hazards and risks as the Australian bus trip or Heyerdahl's voyages. Frequently a trial of a complex undertaking can tell you that a thing is *possible*. That knowledge, like the knowledge gained from Columbus's first voyage, can be of very great value. That is the reason I think a trial of an unlikely undertaking deserves its own name: the method of possibilities. If you think of a case study merely as one case out of the thirty or a hundred you will need to estimate a statistic, that is not what I mean by the method of possibilities. I mean a trial of a course of action to find out whether it might be possible to bring it off.

What Can Be Done?

A great deal of social science is currently devoted to finding out what individuals, pairs, groups, organizations, and other collectivities do *at present*. That is useful. Unfortunately, many social scientists then conclude that they have learned, in the nature of things, what is possible. That is the same mistake most European mariners made before 1492. They saw no ships during their lifetimes sailing off westward into the great Atlantic. "Young man," they said, "if you want to get to someplace worth getting to, don't go west." Social scientists often make similar recommendations. Finding that 70 percent of projects (job enrichment, say) in a study failed to produce the expected result, they advise readers not to try job enrichment to get that result. The chances, they say, are 70 out of 100 that their readers' attempts will fail.

But what about the 30 percent who came close, or the five percent who got even a better result than they had hoped? Were those flukes? No, they were not. Those people were doing something right. The manager who is thinking about job enrichment may not be very interested in those 70 percent who did something wrong. The manager may want to know how to do something right in this one company (how to sail this one ocean). And probabilities do not apply to the single case.

From the viewpoint of control theory, you must be careful about what you mean by a recipe—a design for doing something. A recipe built on control theory will not be a list of inputs; it will not be a list of "stimuli." It will be an arrangement for enabling the environment to contain enough degrees of freedom so that people can act cooperatively and persistently in carrying out their joint task. It will be an arrangement that permits people to pursue the task and their own purposes without treading on one another's feedback loops.

In brief, the method of possibilities is useful for discovering what people *can* do—discovering what they can do that they do not now do, or discovering the extent to which they might come to do routinely what they now do only rarely.

For example, I think it could bring very great profit both to theory and to ordinary life to mount a series of investigations into the ways people in groups can go about finding their way toward committing themselves to cooperative behavior. I know that a great many studies have been published on cooperation. Most of them, in the tradition of the method of relative frequencies, tell us that among sophomores engaged temporarily in a task that has little or no importance in their daily lives, a group working for an hour under certain conditions exhibited more or stronger signs of cooperation (at least to a degree unlikely to have been pure chance) than another group under other conditions. A few studies even report observing the same group under different conditions. I do not know of any study outside the consulting literature (which few respectable psychologists would be caught reading) that shows how a group under natural conditions engaged in work that has fateful consequences can find its way, grope by grope, from competition or individualistic work to cooperative work. Nor do I know of any, even in the consulting literature, that shows how to test a criterion for loopiness. For that, we need the method of specimens.

The consulting literature does contain frequent accounts of trials of new ways of doing things. They usually illustrate the method of possibilities. I gave a couple of actual examples under "Examples" in the first part of this chapter.

Sometimes the studies reported in the literature are done without great care in measurement, and sometimes they do not give me as much detail on the exact steps taken as I would like, but I do not like to look a gift horse in the mouth.

People from many fields of work help us to imagine the possibilities of past, present, and future—people from anthropology, economics, geography, geology, history, linguistics, and many other scientific and scholarly fields. Equally inventive and influential in proposing possibilities, I think, are artists, poets, fiction writers, and other workers in the arts and humanities. All of us participate in the grand and insatiable urge to explain our world and ourselves.

The Method

You cannot discover very many of the things people, groups, or organizations are capable of doing when you sample or even take a census. Since the more remarkable, unexpected things people do appear rarely, you are unlikely to find those things in a sample. When they do appear, you may, if the method of relative frequencies is uppermost in your mind, mistake them for some sort of "error." You may not even find them in a census, because the people may not be doing those things when the interviewer or observer comes by. If you have your heart set on discovering capabilities of persons, groups, or organizations not usually called forth, do not try casting the net. Ask someone, anyone: "Do you know anyone who is doing something like ____?" You will often be surprised at how few people you have to ask before you find someone who knows someone who knows who is doing what you are looking for.

If your purpose is to find out what persons, groups, or organizations *can* do, then you are relieved of some of the restrictions you must suffer when you study what they are doing at present. You do not need stability of characteristics, because you are going to alter some characteristics anyway—actually, you will probably help the person, group, or organization make its own alterations. You do not need a listable population, because the new capability will take the person, group, or organization out of any existing population. I am not sure whether you even need the person, group, or organization to be well bounded.

If you are weary of conducting experiments with the method of relative frequencies on nonrandom samples, turning out results that do not get clearly corroborated or clearly scrapped until someone carries out a meta-analysis, after which your work becomes an anonymous piece of an effect size, and if you cannot afford the cost of random samples, you might consider turning to experiments on what persons, groups, or organizations *can* do.

In the method of possibilities, as Feyerabend (1978) would put it, anything goes.

14

Summary

Theory makes a crucial difference in method. I am not saying merely that theory affects the variables you will choose to control in an experiment or the questions you will choose to put in a questionnaire. I am saying that theory affects the very kinds of events and successions of them that you will believe to be possible and impossible in *any* investigation. Theory decides the nature of the things and events you will generalize about. (If you wish, you may substitute "metatheory" or "assumptions" for "theory" in those sentences.) If you believe there can be such things as independent and dependent variables, generalization will mean one thing to you; if you believe there cannot be, it will mean something else.

If you believe that stimuli are connected in some systematic, regular way to responses, inputs to outputs, if you believe that input conditions can by themselves cause output actions and that output actions do not simultaneously cause inputs, if you believe that people have qualities or traits or attitudes inside them such that "more" or the "stronger" of them make certain actions more likely (or more rapid or intense) or if you believe that stimuli have "strength" or "drive potential" that makes certain actions more likely or rapid or intense, and, in particular, if you believe that you can tell whether you have guessed right about your variables only by counting the people whose actions you predict correctly (almost as if you were counting votes in your favor), then you will be convinced of the logic of the method of relative frequencies.

If you believe, however, that environmental events (stimuli) spur some people to action (are disturbances for some people) and move others not at all, if you believe that of those who are spurred to action, some are acting to maintain one kind of input, some another, and some several, if you believe that internal variables and bodily action are connected not by correlations between the one and the other but by discrepancy between an internal value or level and the value or level of an incoming perception, if you believe that people are never moved to a particular action by either internal motivation or by external disturbance alone, but choose actions as a way to remove threats to perceptions they want to maintain, if you believe it is the interaction between the person's action and some feature of the external environment that produces "input," if you believe that it is the interaction among input, internal standard, and multitudinous features of internal processing that produces "output," and, in particular, if you believe that you can tell when you have guessed right about the perception a person is controlling only by finding a variable that does *not* vary with environmental variations when the person is free to act, then you will want to use the method of specimens and The Test to learn about human behavior.

That is a little overstated, though not much. Casting nets does not require the beliefs I mentioned above in connection with the method of relative frequencies. Indeed, you can have individual feedback loops in mind when you cast a net. Furthermore, each method can serve the other, as I illustrated in Chapter 13 under "Action Research." But I wanted to contrast the methods as they are most often used to investigate the nature of the human creature. I wanted to put in bold relief the beliefs I think the two methods require when used for that purpose.

If you use the method of relative frequencies, you will compare people by classifying them anonymously into cells by auguries and then looking for *differences* between cells on the "dependent variable." If you use The Test, you will look at individual persons and then look for *invariances* from person to person. If you do not know about The Test but are dissatisfied with the method of relative frequencies (as are many clinicians, for example), you will turn to the study of individuals anyway, maybe feeling guilty, defensive, or disreputable as you do so.

I am arguing that the method of specimens is fully as honorable as the method of relative frequencies. The two methods are both valuable scientifically and commercially; they serve different purposes. I do not think I am running much of a risk when I claim that the method of specimens is the one through which we can study psychology. I do not know a good short label to put on what the method of relative frequencies studies (other than "statistics," which sounds more derogatory than the method deserves), but it cannot be psychology in the sense of the nature of the species.

Perhaps the method of specimens still seems strange to you. Short of actually setting yourself to learning to do it, I can think of no better help in learning to think about it than Keller's (1983) *A Feeling for the Organism: The Life and Work of Barbara McClintock.* McClintock studies corn, not people, but to her every corn plant is as individual as our friends are to you and me. "I start with the seedling, and I don't want to leave it. . . . So I know every plant in the field. I know them intimately, and I find it a great pleasure to know them" (p. 198). But that is not to say that each living creature is a universe unto itself. What marks Barbara McClintock as a scientist, Keller says, "is her unwavering confidence in the underlying order of living forms. . . . Cells, and organisms, have an organization of their own in which nothing is random" (pp. 200–201).

DIFFERENCES BETWEEN RELATIVE FREQUENCIES AND SPECIMENS

Maybe the easiest way to remember or symbolize the difference between the method of relative frequencies and the method of specimens is to compare investigating the junk box (described in Chapter 3) with investigating natural kinds (described in Chapter 9). I will now, however, put a few words on some particular techniques in which the method of specimens differs from the method of frequencies.

Randomizing

In the method of specimens, you do not select persons randomly from a population of persons. You use methods that will enable you to predict a constancy, an invariance, at very high percentages of moments—95 or even 98 percent of them. If your first efforts, indeed, do not get you a percentage high enough to make it silly to calculate a statistical significance, you know you must redesign your experiment. You do not assess success by counting proportions of persons. Every person, if you are seeking to understand the functioning of humans as a species, must turn out to function according to the same kind of internal rules—not to show the same kinds of action, but to use the same manner of organization, just as all the persons in Figure 9.1 used the power law to organize their perceptions of differing sound pressures.

Sampling

In the method of specimens, you do not sample people in the sense the term has in the method of relative frequencies. You do not sample acts, because individuals choose acts to serve purposes, not as consummations in themselves. Nor need you sample the disturbances, in any sense of representing a population of them, that get in the way of a purpose.

In the method of specimens, you take frequent samples of moments so as to be sure of the curve you are plotting. In several of Powers's experiments, he sampled the positions at which the subjects were maintaining a cursor on a computer screen every thirty-sixth of a second. Sampling in the method of specimens has the same meaning it has to the engineer who samples sound in digital audio-recording or who samples the patterns of light coming into a tele-vision camera by splitting it into pixels of wave-length and intensity on the screen.

Most experiments in social science examine behavior at instants so far sep-arated that the moment-to-moment dynamics of the developing action cannot be discovered. One of the few happy exceptions is a study of chickens carried out by Chase (1980). He watched continuously for aggressive acts (pecks, feather-pulls, clawings, and jump-ons) among 24 triads of chickens and recorded the split seconds at which 2,801 such acts occurred. He showed that chickens' habits of aggressive acts toward strange chickens must inevitably, if peaceful relations are eventually to occur, result in a perfect or near-perfect transitive pecking order.

Experimental Controls

You do not need "control groups" in the method of specimens, but you do, of course, need to know what is happening in your experiment. If a subject has accepted your request to move a handle to maintain his or her perception that a cursor is moving on a computer screen in a regular pattern, you do not want some internal standard superior to your request to come into play and disrupt the experiment. You do not want someone to yell "Fire!" You do not want to discover that you have scheduled the person too close to the time the person has agreed to meet his or her spouse at a restaurant and may therefore be distracted by that thought. You want to hold constant the internal standard in charge, so to speak, or to be ready to make a record of any change in it. You want the internal standard that is resetting the standards lower down to remain the same one throughout the experiment, or you want to be able to tell exactly when that standard is displaced by another.

You may run some preliminary trials so that the person can become familiar with the setting and the equipment—so that you can establish a baseline. Psy-chophysicists are familiar with this kind of experimental control.

Tracking

In the method of relative frequencies, investigators typically collect data at one moment (or as close to one moment as makes no practical difference) or at a series of widely spaced moments (the latter being known as time-series designs) with no close tracking of behavior between those pretests and post-tests. In the method of specimens, the continuous moment-to-moment behav-ior, without appreciable gaps, is the crucial behavior to watch. You look for lawfulness in behavior by watching for the continuing regularity in it from moment to moment. When you come upon a feature of environmental input that the person must be perceiving as constant while the person's perceptions of other things must be changing, then you have learned something about internal organization—and causation.

Precision

Precision in the method of relative frequencies is chiefly a matter of the confidence interval. You narrow the confidence interval and increase your confidence in it by finding a population that changes only slowly, by following strictly the rules of random sampling, and by selecting a larger sample. Those matters have much greater effect on success in casting a net than precision of measurement of variables. I wish I knew the name of the clever person who produced this triplet:

Measure it with a micrometer.
Mark it with a crayon.
Cut it with an axe.

Precision in the method of specimens is chiefly a matter of using techniques of measurement that are at least as precise as the precision of control the person (the "subject") can exert. At the lower levels of the neural hierarchy, human control of action can be very precise indeed. The reason for wanting precise measurement is to be sure that unexpected lack of control by the person is indeed due to the person and is a signal that you have not yet found the right internal standard—to be sure that the apparent lack of control is not due to loose joints in your measuring instruments.

A good model of human functioning should even predict correctly the degree of failure of the human to match the incoming perception exactly to the internal standard—the amount of error in the person's compensating actions. In an unpublished paper entitled "Hierarchical Control in Human Performance," Marken and Powers have reported building a working model that did that. When they reversed the connection between environmental events and the variable the subject wanted to control, the model made the same quantitative degree of error before adjusting to the new connection that the human subjects did.

Sometimes it takes us a long time to reach a goal. If a book is not now in its place on the library shelf, we look for it a few feet in either direction, ask the librarian if it is waiting to be shelved, fill out a reserve card, and then wait a week. Investigating the higher-level internal standards will be more difficult than investigating the lower-level ones because of the time it may take for the person to reduce error in the perceptual input. The behavior must be tracked until the error gets to zero or close to it. The question of what we can mean by precision in the method of specimens when searching for higher-level internal standards seems to me a nasty one.

Having summarized my point of view in what I said above, I will now summarize quickly the uses of the research methods I have described in this book.

RELATIVE FREQUENCIES

Both the methods of relative frequencies and of specimens are very valuable. The method of relative frequencies helps you find things. You can cast a net to discover whether there is a greater density of what you are looking for (perhaps people who want to vote for Candlebrass, perhaps people who arrive at work on time more often than others) in certain parts of the country, among people who get high scores on ethnocentrism, among people who step off the curb at a traffic light after the "Don't Walk" sign comes on, and so on. The method of relative frequencies is the only method we have for casting nets effectively, but that need give us no worry; it is indeed very effective. Furthermore, if you use the method properly, you can make a good estimate of how confident you should be in the information you pull in. And the method tells you exactly how to design your net to have whatever level of confidence in your catch you may wish.

The method also enables you to catalog the current kinds of behavior to be found in any specified population. A series of such catalogs can be the stuff of history. They can be used to plot trends of great value to business people, economists, politicians, public health workers, educators, and others.

The method cannot tell you anything about the nature of the individual creature, about the nature of the species. It cannot find invariants for you.

SPECIMENS

The method of specimens looks for invariants. It can find the kind of functioning that you will see in every human. It can find the hierarchical control of experience in the individual and the invariants of that hierarchy in the species. The method is not good for casting a net, cataloging varieties of behavior in a population, or writing history.

ACTION RESEARCH

A combination of the methods of relative frequencies and specimens is especially effective in research on behavior in particular organized collectivities of people. It is especially effective, too, for consultants helping members of organizations to change the way they coordinate their efforts. The combination method is generally known as "action research."

POSSIBILITIES

Finally, simply finding out whether it is possible to do something can be very valuable. The single trial is a method familiar and useful to workaday researchers, but often disdained by formal researchers devoted to the method of relative frequencies. Unlike the methods of relative frequencies and specimens, the method of possibilities has no rules.

I am not saying that the method of possibilities requires that the tactics or rules of the other methods actually be avoided. If, for example, you are carrying out a single trial of a way of coordinating effort in an organization, it is often a good idea to follow the method of action research, which requires following the rules of the two methods of relative frequencies and specimens when you use them. But even then, if those rules get in your way, push them aside. The only rule in the method of possibilities is "Try it!"—despite any rules that other people may like to follow.

NOW WHAT?

To researchers in social science who seek zealously the human nature, I propose that it is time to turn to methods—and to their corresponding theories—that can enable us to predict correctly at least 98 percent of the time. It is time, too, to give up trying to predict particular, outwardly observable acts and to study instead the perceptual consequences of acts, unpredictable though the acts themselves may be. It is time to cease substituting what one subject did in an experiment for evidence of what another subject did. It is time to stop relying as heavily as we do on what subjects tell us and what we tell the subjects. It is time to give up the assumption of linear input-output causation and adopt instead the assumption of circular causation in feedback loops. It is time to investigate the control of perception.

The term "generalizing" has a clear and useful meaning within the method of relative frequencies when we want to predict proportions in samples taken from a listed population. The concept works well in extrapolating from a statistic in one sample to that same sort of statistic in another. In looking for the rules of internal functioning of the human creature, however, I do not believe that generalizing can have a useful meaning unless we can tell what a particular person will do, not what an average over a hundred people will look like. If we cannot point to any one particular person and show that our description of behavior can be seen in that person's actions, then I do not think we can make the claim that our description is generalizable—that it is true "in general." I know that many social scientists maintain that their science is properly concerned only with generalities and should take no interest in the behavior of any particular person. But I myself cannot understand what "generalizing" or "in general" can mean unless it applies to the particular.

It is time, after a hundred years, that we give up trying to make the method of relative frequencies do what it cannot do.

My summary of my summary is this: Use a method to do what it *can* do. Do not try to make it do what it cannot. No one method is good for everything. But every method is good for doing something worth doing.

I wish you success in doing it.

References

Aoki, Ted T. (1984). Interests, knowledge, and evaluation: Alternative curriculum evaluation orientations. In T. T. Aoki (Ed.), *Curriculum evaluation in a new key.* Edmonton, Alberta, Canada: Department of Secondary Education, Faculty of Education, University of Alberta.

Baum, W. M., Hayne W. Reese, and W. T. Powers (1973). Behaviorism and feedback control. (An exchange of letters.) *Science*, 181(4105), 1116, 1118–20.

Bem, Daryl J., and Andrea Allen (1974). On predicting some of the people some of the time: The search for cross-situational consistencies in behavior. *Psychological Review*, 81(6), 506–20.

Bohannan, Paul, W. T. Powers, and Mark Schoepfle (1974). Systems conflict in the learning alliance. In L. J. Stiles (Ed.), *Theories for teaching*, pp. 76–96. New York: Dodd, Mead.

Breger, L., and C. Ruiz (1966). The role of ego-defense in conformity. *Journal of Social Psychology*, 69, 73–85.

Bronfenbrenner, Urie (1958). Socialization and social class through time and space. In E. E. Maccoby, T. M. Newcomb, and E. L. Hartley (Eds.), *Readings in social psychology*, pp. 400–424. New York: Holt, Rinehart, and Winston. Condensed in H. Proshansky and B. Seidenberg (Eds.), *Basic studies in social psychology*, pp. 349–65. New York: Holt, Rinehart, and Winston.

Brown, Daniel J. (1975). Mirror, mirror. . . . Down with the linear model. *American Educational Research Journal*, 12(4), 491–505.

Brown, J. Larry (1987). Hunger in the U.S. *Scientific American*, 256(2), 37–41.

Bullock, R. J., and Daniel J. Svyantek (1987). The impossibility of using random strategies to study the organization development process. *Journal of Applied Behavioral Science* 23(2), 255–62.

Cairns, Robert B. (1986). Phenomena lost: Issues in the study of development. In Jaan Valsiner (Ed.), *The individual subject and scientific psychology*, pp. 97–111. New York: Plenum.

Chase, Ivan D. (1980). Social process and hierarchy formation in small groups: A comparative perspective. *American Sociological Review*, 45(6), 905–24.

Cook, Stuart W. (1987). The origins of action research. *SAFT Newsletter* (of the Society for the Advancement of Field Theory), 1 (3, Summer), 1–2.

Corder-Bolz, Charles R. (1978). *A Monte Carlo study of six models of change.* Research paper No. 1-02-78. Austin, Tex.: Southwest Educational Development Laboratory.

Cotton, John L., and Jeffrey M. Tuttle (1986). Employee turnover: A meta-analysis and review with implications for research. *Academy of Management Review*, 11(1), 55–70.

Cronbach, Lee J. (1975). Beyond the two disciplines of scientific psychology. *American Psychologist*, 30, 116–27.

Dember, W. N., and Robert W. Earl (1957). Analysis of exploratory, manipulatory, and curiosity behaviors. *Psychological Review*, 64, 91–96.

Dember, W. N., and Joel S. Warm (1979). *Psychology of perception*, 2nd ed. New York: Holt, Rinehart, and Winston.

Dember, W. N., Robert W. Earl, and N. Paradise (1957). Response by rats to differential stimulus complexity. *Journal of Comparative and Physiological Psychology*, 50, 514–18.

Edwards, Ward (1961). Costs and payoffs are instructions. *Psychological Review*, 68, 275–84.

Feyerabend, Paul (1978). *Against method.* London: Verso; New York: Schocken Books.

Franck, Isaac (1986). Psychology as a science: Resolving the idiographic-nomothetic controversy. In Jaan Valsiner (Ed.), *The individual subject and scientific psychology*, pp. 17–36. New York: Plenum.

Frey, Dieter, and Dagmar Stahlberg (1986). Selection of information after receiving more or less reliable self-threatening information. *Personality and Social Psychology Bulletin*, 12(4), 434–41.

Fricke, Benno G. (1956). Prediction, selection, mortality, and quality control. *College and University*, 32, 34–52.

Gergen, Kenneth J. (1973). Social psychology as history. *Journal of Personality and Social Psychology*, 26(2), 309–20.

Gergen, Kenneth J., and Jill Morawski (1980). An alternative metatheory for social psychology. In L. Wheeler (Ed.), *Review of personality and social psychology: 1.* Beverly Hills, Calif.: Sage.

Gordon, Michael E., L. Allen Slade, and Neal Schmitt (1986). The "science of the sophomore" revisited: From conjecture to empiricism. *Academy of Management Review*, 11(1), 191–207.

Gottfredson, Gary D. (1981). School and delinquency. In S. E. Martin, L. B. Sechrest, and R. Redner (Eds.), *New directions in the rehabilitation of criminal offenders*, pp. 424–69. Washington, D.C.: National Academy Press.

Grossman, Klaus E. (1986). From idiographic approaches to nomothetic hypotheses. In

Jaan Valsiner (Ed.), *The individual subject and scientific psychology*, pp. 37–69. New York: Plenum.

Hackman, J. Richard (1985). Doing research that makes a difference. In E. E. Lawler III and associates, *Doing research that is useful for theory and practice*. San Francisco: Jossey-Bass.

Hershberger, Wayne A. (Ed.) (1989). *Volitional action: Conation and control*. Amsterdam: Elsevier/North Holland.

Kaplan, Robert E., Michael M. Lombardo, and Mignon S. Mazique (1985). A mirror for managers: Using simulation to develop management teams. *Journal of Applied Behavioral Science* 21(3), 241–53.

Keller, Evelyn Fox (1983). *A feeling for the organism: The life and work of Barbara McClintock*. New York: W. H. Freeman.

Koslowsky, Meni, and Gardner Locke (1986). Decision rules for increasing the rate of successfully classified respondents. *Journal of Applied Behavioral Science*, 22(2), 187–93.

Krech, David, and Richard S. Crutchfield (1948). *Theory and problems of social psychology*. New York: McGraw-Hill.

Lindblom, Charles E., and David K. Cohen (1979). *Usable knowledge: Social science and social problem solving*. New Haven, Conn.: Yale University Press.

Luthans, Fred, Stuart A. Rosenkrantz, and Harry W. Hennessey (1985). What do successful managers really do? An observation study of managerial activities. *Journal of Applied Behavioral Science*, 21(3), 255–70.

Mace, F. Charles, and Thomas R. Kratochwill (1986). The individual subject in behavioral analysis research. In Jaan Valsiner (Ed.), *The individual subject and scientific psychology*, pp. 153–80. New York: Plenum.

McGrath, Joseph E., and Irwin Altman (1966). *Small group research: A synthesis and critique of the field*. New York: Holt, Rinehart, and Winston.

McGuigan, F. J. (1963). The experimenter: A neglected stimulus object. *Psychological Bulletin*, 60, 421–28.

MacIntyre, Alasdair (1984). *After virtue*. Notre Dame, Ind.: Notre Dame University Press.

Marken, Richard S. (1980). The cause of control movements in a tracking task. *Perceptual and Motor Skills*, 51, 755–58.

——— (1982). Intentional and accidental behavior: A control theory analysis. *Psychological Reports*, 50, 647–50.

——— (1983). "Mind reading": A look at changing intentions. *Psychological Reports*, 53, 267–70.

——— (1985). Selection of consequences: Adaptive behavior from random reinforcement. *Psychological Reports*, 56, 379–83.

——— (1986). Perceptual organization of behavior: A hierarchical control model of coordinated action. *Journal of Experimental Psychology: Human Perception and Performance*, 12(3), 267–76.

——— (1988). The nature of behavior: Control as fact and theory. *Behavioral Science*, 33, 196–206.

Meyerhoff, Michael K., and Burton L. White (1986). Making the grade as parents. *Psychology Today*, 20(9), 38, 42–45.

Miller, George A., Eugene Galanter, and Karl H. Pribram (1960). *Plans and the structure of behavior*. New York: Holt.

Miller, James G. (1978). *Living systems*. New York: McGraw-Hill.

Mohandessi, K., and Philip J. Runkel (1958). Some socio-economic correlates of academic aptitude. *Journal of Educational Psychology*, 49, 47–52.

Orne, M. T. (1962). On the social psychology of the psychological experiment: With particular reference to demand characteristics and their implications. *American Psychologist*, 17, 776–83.

Perrow, Charles (1978). Demystifying organizations. In R. C. Saari and Y. Hasenfeld (Eds.), *The management of human services*, pp. 105–20. New York: Columbia University Press.

Phillips, Deborah A. (1987). Inventing human nature. *Contemporary Psychology*, 32(10), 853–54. A review of Lynette Friedrich-Cofer (Ed.), *Human nature and public policy: Scientific views of women, children, and families*. New York: Praeger, 1986.

Powers, Mary (1987). To Michael Yocum. (Letter to the editor.) *Continuing the Conversation: A Newsletter of Ideas in Cybernetics*, 10 (Fall), 15.

Powers, W. T. (1971). A feedback model for behavior: Application to a rat experiment. *Behavioral Science*, 16(6), 558–63.

——— (1973a). Feedback: Beyond behaviorism. *Science*, 179(4071), 351–56.

——— (1973b). *Behavior: The control of perception*. New York: Aldine.

——— (1975). Review of "The Logic of Social Systems" by A. Kuhn. *Contemporary Sociology*, 4(2), 92–94.

——— (1976). Control-system theory and performance objectives. *Journal of Psycholinguistic Research*, 5(3), 285–97.

——— (1977). Feedback principles in behavioral organization. In H. Zeier (Ed.), *Psychology of the 20th century, Volume 4: Pawlow und die Folgen*, pp. 573–613. Zurich: Kindler-Verlag. In German.

——— (1978). Quantitative analysis of purposive systems: Some spadework at the foundations of scientific psychology. *Psychological Review*, 85(5), 417–35.

——— (1979a). Degrees of freedom in social interaction. In K. Krippendorf (Ed.), *Communication and control in society*, pp. 267–78. New York: Gordon and Breach.

——— (1979b). A cybernetic model for research in human development. In M. N. Ozer (Ed.), *A cybernetic approach to the assessment of children: Toward a more humane use of human beings*, pp. 11–66. Boulder, Colo.: Westview.

——— (1979c). The nature of robots, Part I: Defining behavior. *Byte*, 4(6), 132–34, 136, 138, 140–41, 144. Part II: Simulated control system. *Byte*, 4(7), 134–36, 138, 140, 142, 144, 146, 148–50. Part III: A closer look at human behavior. *Byte*, 4(8), 94–96, 98, 100, 102–104, 106–108, 110–12, 114, 116. Part IV: Looking for controlled variables. *Byte*, 4(9), 96, 98–102, 104, 106–10, 112.

——— (1980). A systems approach to consciousness. In J. M. Davidson and R. J. Davidson (Eds.), *The psychobiology of consciousness*, pp. 217–42. New York: Plenum.

——— (1987). *Control theory: A new look at human behavior*. Scottsdale, Ariz.: Control System Group (10209 North 56th Street, 85253). Four VHS cassette tapes.

——— (1989). *Living control systems: Selected papers of William T. Powers*. Gravel Switch, Ky.: Control Systems Group, Inc.

Powers, W. T., R. K. Clark, and R. L. McFarland (1960). A general feedback theory of human behavior, Part I. *Perceptual and Motor Skills*, 11(1), Monograph Supplement, 71–88. Part II, 11(3), Monograph Supplement, 309–23. Part I reprinted in L. von Bertalanffy and A. Rapoport (Eds.), *General systems: Yearbook of the Society for General Systems Research*, vol. 5, pp. 63–73, Part II on pp. 75–83. Ann Arbor, Mich. Society for General Systems Research. Part I reprinted in A. G. Smith (Ed.), *Communication and culture: Readings in the codes of human interaction*, pp. 333–43. New York: Holt, Rinehart, and Winston, 1966.

Robertson, Richard J., David M. Goldstein, Michael Mermel, and Melanie Musgrave (1987). Testing the self as a control system: Theoretical and methodological issues. Unpublished paper, Department of Psychology, Northeastern Illinois University.

Rosenthal, Robert (1967). *Experimenter effects in behavioral research*. New York: Appleton-Century-Crofts.

Runkel, Philip J., and Joseph E. McGrath (1972). *Research on human behavior: A systematic guide to method*. New York: Holt, Rinehart, and Winston.

Runkel, Philip J., Spencer H. Wyant, Warren E. Bell, and Margaret Runkel (1980). *Organizational renewal in a school district: Self-help through a cadre of organizational specialists*. Eugene, Oreg.: Center for Educational Policy and Management, University of Oregon.

Schlesinger, G. (1967). Natural kinds. In R. S. Cohen and M. W. Wartofsky (Eds.), *Boston Studies in the Philosophy of Science*, vol. 3, pp. 108–22. Dordrecht, The Netherlands: Reidel.

Schmuck, Richard A., and Philip J. Runkel (1985). *Handbook of organization development in schools*, 3d ed. Palo Alto, Calif.: Mayfield.

Schoonhoven, Claudia Bird (1981). Problems with contingency theory: Testing assumptions hidden within the language of contingency "theory." *Administrative Science Quarterly*, 26(3), 349–77.

Schumacher, E. F. (1973). *Small is beautiful: Economics as if people mattered*. London: Blond and Briggs.

Schwartz, Stephen P. (Ed.) (1977). *Naming, necessity, and natural kinds*. Ithaca, N.Y.: Cornell University Press.

Sherif, Muzafer, O. J. Harvey, B. J. White, W. R. Hood, and Carolyn W. Sherif (1961). *Intergroup conflict and cooperation: The Robbers Cave experiment*. Norman, Okla.: Institute of Group Relations, University of Oklahoma. Recounted in Chapter 9 of Muzafer Sherif and Carolyn W. Sherif (1956). *Outline of social psychology*, rev. ed. New York: Harper; and in Chapter 11 of Muzafer Sherif and Carolyn W. Sherif (1969). *Social Psychology*. New York: Harper and Row.

Smith, Thomas J., and Karl U. Smith (1988). The cybernetic basis of human behavior and performance. *Continuing the Conversation: A Newsletter of Ideas in Cybernetics*. 15 (Winter 1988), 1–28.

Stevens, S. S., and M. Guirao (1964). Individual loudness functions. *Journal of the Acoustical Society of America* 36, 2210–13.

Szamosi, Geza (1986). *The twin dimensions: Inventing time and space*. New York: McGraw-Hill.

Thorngate, Warren (1986). The production, detection, and explanation of behavioral patterns. In Jaan Valsiner (Ed.), *The individual subject and scientific psychology*, 71–93. New York: Plenum.

Tyler, Leona E. (1983). *Thinking creatively: A new approach to psychology and individual lives*. San Francisco: Jossey-Bass.

Valsiner, Jaan (1986). Between groups and individuals: Psychologists' and laypersons' interpretations of correlational findings. In Jaan Valsiner (Ed.), *The individual subject and scientific psychology*, pp. 113–51. New York: Plenum.

van de Rijt-Plooij, Hetty H. C., and Franz X. Plooij (1986). The involvement of interactional processes and hierarchical systems control in the growing independence in chimpanzee infancy. In J. Wind and V. Reynolds (Eds.), *Essays in human sociobiology*, vol. 2, pp. 155–65. Brussels: V. U. B. Press, Study Series No. 26.

Webb, Eugene J., and others (1966). *Unobtrusive measures: Nonreactive research in the social sciences*. Chicago: Rand McNally.

Weisbord, Marvin R. (1987a). Toward third-wave managing and consulting. *Organizational Dynamics*, 15(3), 5–24.

——— (1987b). *Productive workplaces: Organizing and managing for dignity, meaning, and community*. San Francisco: Jossey-Bass.

Williams, William D. (1986). Control theory and the Smithian economics. *Continuing the Conversation: A Newsletter of Ideas in Cybernetics*, 7 (Winter), 14–17.

Winne, Philip H. (1983). Distortions of construct validity in multiple regression analysis. *Canadian Journal of Behavioral Science*, 15(3), 187–202.

Name Index

Subject Index

ABOUT THE AUTHOR

PHILIP J. RUNKEL is Professor Emeritus of Education and of Psychology at the University of Oregon. For 35 years, he has taught and written in the fields of social psychology, school organization, research method, statistics, and organizational consulting. His work as an organizational consultant to schools began in 1968. His publications include *Research on Human Behavior: A Systematic Guide to Method* (with Joseph E. McGrath), *Handbook of Organization Development in Schools* (3rd edition, with Richard A. Schmuck), several other books, and several dozen articles and chapters.

M...

As I said ...
is too simple to se...
In the next chapter, you will con...
gram—Figure 11.6. It exemplifies a diagram that can serve ...
eling. It illustrates how a more complex system must ...
tions and hierarchies and more complex interconnec...
one would expect to see in a mode...
In Chapter 11
an experiment ...
provide t...

of c...
We con...
b...